A Handbook
for
ESL Literacy

Jill Bell

Barbara Burnaby

OISE PRESS

in association with

HODDER & STOUGHTON LIMITED

The Ontario Institute for Studies in Education has three prime functions: to conduct programs of graduate study in education, to undertake research in education, and to assist in the implementation of the findings of educational studies. The institute is a college chartered by an Act of the Ontario Legislature in 1965. It is affiliated with the University of Toronto for graduate studies purposes.

The publications program of the Institute has been established to make available information and materials arising from studies in education, to foster the spirit of critical inquiry, and to provide a forum for the exchange of ideas about education. The opinions expressed should be viewed as those of the contributors.

© The Ontario Institute for Studies in Education 1984
  252 Bloor Street West,
  Toronto, Ontario
  M5S 1V6

Published by OISE Press in association with Hodder & Stoughton Limited. Distributed by Pippin Publishing Limited, 380 Esna Park Drive, Markham, Ontario L3R 1H5.

Canadian Cataloguing in Publication Data

Bell, Jill, 1946-
  A handbook for ESL literacy

Bibliography: p.
ISBN 0-7744-0270-9 (OISE)
ISBN 0-340-35709-7 (Hodder & Stoughton)

1. English language — Study and teaching — Non-English-speaking students.* 2. Adult education. I. Burnaby, Barbara J., 1943-   II. Title.

PE1128.A2B44 1984   428'.007   C84-098214-3

First published 1984
Reprinted 1985
Reprinted 1986
Reprinted 1988
Reprinted 1990
Reprinted 1993

Printed in Canada by Hignell Printing Limited

Contents

Acknowledgements

This book was developed in the Modern Language Centre of the Ontario Institute for Studies in Education. The project was funded through the Ontario Ministry of Education transfer grants to OISE.

We are grateful to the following people who reviewed the manuscript and in other ways contributed ideas and materials to the book: Michelle Burtoff, Center for Applied Linguistics; Tracy Carpenter, Frontier College; Rosalind Elson, Ontario Ministry of Citizenship and Culture; Brenda Duncombe, St. Stephen's Community House; Chris Fraser, Scadding Court Community Centre; Ian Gertsbain, George Brown College (particularly exercises on pages 58 and 98); Bonita Greenbaum, North York Board of Education; Jean Handscombe, North York Board of Education; Pia Moriarty, San Francisco, California (particularly material on page 26); Pat Morrison, Toronto; Donna Payne, English in the Workplace; Sidney Pratt, Ontario Ministry of Citizenship and Culture; Julie Reid, Toronto Board of Education; Kay Robinson, Toronto; Virginia Sauvé, Alberta Vocational Centre; Kathleen Troy, Mohawk College; Jean Unda, St. Christopher House; Annette Vafa, North York Public Library; and members of the staffs of East End Literacy, the YWCA, the Citizenship Interagency Project, and the Centre for Labour Studies at Humber College. We are greatly indebted to many people for their help and we apologize to anyone whose contribution has inadvertently not been acknowledged here. Any errors or omissions in the text are fault of the authors and not of those who have so generously given us their time and ideas.

Introduction

This handbook is intended to provide a practical guide to the teaching of initial reading and writing skills to adult students whose first language is not English. It is hoped that it will be useful as a resource for practising literacy teachers and also as background to the field for teachers in training.

The need for literacy training for non-English-speaking adults, has been highlighted in recent years by the influx of refugees from Southeast Asia, considerable numbers of whom speak languages for which there is no written form and have therefore never had any exposure to literacy. The problem is by no means restricted to the refugees, however. Of Canadian residents whose first language is neither English nor French, 88.9% have less than a grade 8 education,[1] which is normally considered the minimum for functional literacy, or sufficient reading and writing skills to cope with daily life. This refers of course to first-language literacy, and we can safely assume that the proportion of functional literacy in English is even less.

Obviously most of these people coped with daily life perfectly well prior to their arrival in North America. They may have lived in communities where print was unknown, and never been faced by street signs, posters, and newspapers. Or they may have lived in societies where any reading and writing which had to be done was handled for the entire community by one or two chosen people. In North America, however, society is based on the premise that all individuals can read and write. Finding one's way around becomes dependent on one's ability to read street signs, recognize bus numbers, and read subway names. Government communicates with individuals almost entirely in print. Literacy is usually a prerequisite for promotion to any position with supervisory responsibilities. Health care demands written application

1. Canada, House of Commons, *Work for Tomorrow: Employment Opportunities for the '80s*. Report of the Parliamentary Task Force on Employment Opportunities (Allmand Report). Ottawa: Speaker of the House of Commons, 1981.

forms. Even food shopping requires the ability to differentiate a bag of flour from a bag of sugar by the lettering on the label. Because of these and similar demands, many immigrants who never previously felt a need for literacy find that their life in North America is very limited without reading and writing skills. ESL literacy students are not always recent arrivals, however. Some students have lived in this country for a number of years, relying on a support network of family or colleagues to handle any necessary reading or writing. When this network breaks down, perhaps because a spouse dies or children marry and leave home, the need for literacy training suddenly becomes urgent.

Although a considerable amount of material has been published on the ways in which students learn to read and write, the bulk of research has been based on children learning in their native language. Teachers of ESL literacy to adults need to consider the ways in which the maturity of adult students affects their learning, and the ways in which literacy in a second language is different from mother-tongue literacy. It is obvious, for instance, that adult learners have a depth of experience and maturity of approach to bring to the task of learning to read and write. This advantage, however, may be offset by the added burden of trying to learn literacy skills in a language which has not necessarily been conquered orally. Teachers in adult ESL literacy programs need methods which capitalize on the maturity and motivation of the adult while minimizing the difficulties presented by a second language.

This handbook attempts to demonstrate ways in which teachers can best handle these demands. The bulk of the handbook is concerned with practical teaching methodology and includes sections on content of lessons, teaching approaches, and assessment, with detailed sample lesson sequences illustrating the ways in which these can be combined in the classroom. Also included is some background on second-language literacy, providing the theory on which the suggested methodology is based. This material is written in non-technical language and does not presuppose any prior knowledge of the field.

Although the handbook concentrates on reading and writing skills in the ESL classroom, there is no doubt that the development of oral skills is crucial in attacking literacy in a second language. For this reason, and because literacy students are commonly found in general ESL classes where other students expect equal attention to be paid to listening and speaking, we have, wherever feasible, indicated the ways in which reading and writing activities can be combined with oral work. Second-language literacy students are normally attempting, simultaneously, both to become literate and to improve their oral English, and wherever possible the teacher should devise activities which integrate these skills and help to further both goals.

1 / Literacy Students and Literacy Classes

TYPES OF STUDENTS

Teachers of adult programs in ESL and literacy usually find that their students vary a great deal. As well as the obvious factor of the degree of competence in the English language, they find that students' progress is affected by their length of time in the country, their native language, their age, and their previous experience with education. This last factor is particularly relevant to the ESL literacy teacher. Students who can read and write in their native language are obviously going to find literacy in English a much easier task than students who have never learned to read and write in any language. Generally, students with literacy skills in their native language find it easy to transfer those skills to a second language. We are likely to find that the range of native-language literacy displayed in the ESL literacy class is from zero to barely functional literacy — that is, the ability to use print for survival purposes. A similar range of skills is likely to be evident in the students' abilities to read and write in English, and of course students will not necessarily have equal abilities in both languages.

Because there are many factors affecting students' progress in learning to read and write English, it can be helpful when assessing their needs to consider them as falling into one or more of the following groups.

Students who are illiterate

Students who are illiterate normally have had a maximum of two or three years' schooling in the native language. While they may be able to copy letters and even form some themselves, they do not have any understanding of the concept that a given sound will be represented by a particular letter or combination of letters (sound-symbol cor-

3

respondence). Illiterate students may be subdivided further into *non-literates*, who speak a language for which there is a written form and therefore probably grew up surrounded by newspapers, street signs, and so on, and *pre-literates*, who speak a language for which there is no written form. Such people have had little exposure to print and may even have difficulty in recognizing that a picture represents a real-life object.

- **Tsab** is a man of 35 who came to Canada as a refugee. His home was in the mountains of Laos and he belonged to the Hmong group. The Hmong language has no formalized writing system although, in recent years, work has been done on writing Hmong in the roman alphabet and the Lao script. Tsab's village was a farming community with no local school. All his learning was acquired orally from older adults in the village and he and his fellow villagers never had to use print in their daily lives.

  As the war in Laos progressed, he and his family were forced down from the mountains into refugee camps. Tsab was too old to be eligible for the schools in the camps although he did pick up a fair command of spoken Lao, the language used in the schools. Later he was moved to a refugee camp in Thailand where he learned some Thai.

  When Tsab was finally resettled in Canada he was able to speak three languages but still had no exposure to literacy. With his proven facility for languages Tsab was confident that he could learn English and do well in Canada. He made rapid progress in spoken English but now realizes that this is not sufficient to get him a well-paying job because he will need literacy skills. He is in an ESL class which reflects his oral abilities, but is lagging badly behind the rest of the class in written work.

Students who are semi-literate

Semi-literate students may have had up to eight years of formal education, although sometimes with sporadic attendance for reasons such as family responsibilities or ill health. They understand, even if imperfectly, that the written word relates to the spoken word, but they do not have the skills to attack new words. Normally they lack study skills, and tend to avoid reading or writing whenever possible.

- **Anna** is a 45-year-old woman from the Azores who works as a cleaner in a hospital. She attended school up to grade 4. She came to Canada nearly twenty years ago and has developed a fair competence in spoken English, although she makes a lot of mistakes. She goes to ESL classes two evenings a week in a program which offers basic or advanced-level classes. She is currently in her second year in the basic class because she feels the advanced-level class will be too difficult for her minimal writing skills.

Any reading or writing which she needs is done for her by her children. She would like to learn to read and write so that she can help her children in school but doubts that she has the ability ever to learn.

- **Ella** is a Native Indian woman from an isolated Native community in northern Canada — so isolated that it can only be reached by plane. Everyone in her community speaks her Native language for most purposes. Virtually the only place where English is used is in the school. Ella went to school in her community and completed grade 8. In order to go to high school, Ella was flown out to a small city 600 km from her home. She was boarded with some non-Native people there. There were not many Native students in the school and she knew only three of those. City life was completely new to her. After ten days she got her parents to fly her back home because she was frightened and homesick.

  Several years later Ella married a non-Native pilot. She had two children. The family moved out to a small town 150 km from her community. After a year and a half, her husband left her. In order to get any support other than welfare, Ella needs more literacy skills. While her conversational English is limited, she can get by in speech. But the literacy skills she learned in school have deteriorated because she has had little reason to use them.

Functionally non-literate students

Students who are functionally non-literate have basic literacy skills in their own language which give them the concepts of word and sentences. They may know survival sight-words such as road signs and washroom labels, and any vocabulary specific to their job. They may be able to take or leave simple messages, but they rarely read for pleasure and avoid expressing themselves in writing. They are probably unable to fill out forms or follow written instructions competently.

- **Rosa** is a middle-aged woman from Argentina who stayed at school until she was fourteen. She worked as a hairdresser when she was in Argentina, but has stayed home with her children since she came to Canada fourteen years ago. She reads photo story magazines in Spanish and writes short letters home to her parents occasionally. She has recently got a job as a waitress, and has little trouble understanding her customers although her spoken English is rather fractured. She can read the restaurant menu and has enough written English to fill in the order forms for the kitchen, but otherwise avoids reading and writing in English.

Non-roman alphabetic students

Students whose native language is not written in the roman alphabet will have special difficulties in learning literacy in English no matter how competent their native-language literacy may be. They may fall into any of the above categories, or they may be like the student described below.

- **Ali** is a 32-year-old successful businessman from the Middle East. He is well educated and is used to expressing himself in writing. He has come to Canada with a view to further study, but first must learn English. He has had very little experience with the roman alphabet but he possesses all the reading skills developed in his native language.

PLACING LITERACY STUDENTS IN CLASSES

As we see from these profiles, ESL literacy students are likely to be quite varied in background, education, and language competence. They are likely to have different aims in mind for the class too. Perhaps they want only sufficient literacy to enable them to cope with a cheque book or pass a driver's test. Maybe they want to be able to read stories to their children, or help them with their homework. They may want to go on to Adult Basic Education or even further education. Deciding what is a realistic aim for our students is obviously affected by their current competence and the length of time which they are able to spend on literacy. Few teachers are fortunate enough to have a class of students all at the same level, all keen to be literate.

A more common situation is a varied group of ESL students in which two or three persons are having problems joining in class activities because their reading and writing skills lag far behind their oral ability. Placing these students in a lower-level class does not solve the problem, because their oral skills are too good for the spoken activities in the easier class. In larger institutions the ideal solution is that students of all levels who need special literacy help are withdrawn from the regular classes, either on a part-time basis for literacy instruction or for a special literacy course, after which they return to their regular classrooms. In many places, however, there are not enough students needing literacy training to justify the assignment of a teacher to a special literacy class. It may be possible to refer students elsewhere for literacy training, either to a course run by a larger institution or to the one-on-one tutoring provided by many volunteer organizations. Problems also arise, however, when ESL students are placed in a regular adult literacy class intended for native speakers of English. While the English-speaking students will find the task of reading and writing difficult, they will have a depth of vocabulary and control of sentence patterns which is

not available to the ESL student. Many of the literacy teaching techniques building on similarities between words will bring up vocabulary unknown to the second-language student. Techniques of word attack such as sounding-out words will also be less successful if the student cannot recognize a word even when the correct sounds are formed. Generally, the teacher of native speakers will begin with the assumption that the text will be meaningful to the students once they have sounded out the letters correctly. Unfortunately, this is frequently not true for second-language learners.

ESL literacy students therefore fall between two stools. Their lack of English language skills makes literacy classes difficult. Their lack of literacy makes ESL language classes difficult. They are attempting to cope with two challenges simultaneously — learning the language, and learning how to read and write.

This is not necessarily a problem for the teacher if the students are all at more or less the same level, as the literacy work can grow out of the oral language as students learn it. The teacher of a mixed-level class has a more difficult task. Obviously the needs of the students who cannot read or write should not be ignored, but the teacher's problem is to meet these needs without shortchanging the other students. There are a number of options to be considered. As suggested above, it may be possible to find an ESL literacy class to which the students can be transferred, or they can be referred to agencies providing one-on-one tutoring for extra help. Perhaps a volunteer or teacher aide could come in for part of the class to work exclusively with the students who need literacy training. The most likely option, however, is that the teacher will fall back on the judicious use of group activities. One of the advantages of literacy teaching is that there are numerous useful activities which a student can work on alone, unlike the oral ESL situation where a student needs help with spoken skills and desperately needs a partner with whom to practise. Most well-planned reading and writing activities at any level build on oral work in which the class as a whole has participated. It is usually fairly easy to devise literacy activities which utilize some of the features of this oral work, and which some students can work on alone while the teacher is setting up other reading and writing activities for the rest of the class. This book contains a number of suggestions for ways in which this can be done, particularly in section 3, Teaching Multi-level Classes.

2 / Background to Literacy Theory

READING THEORY

We use the word *reading* to refer to many different skills. Think of the various things you have read today and the different ways in which you read them. Perhaps you glanced at the mail, looked up the time of a bus in the transit schedule, read a couple of chapters of a light novel, and struggled through a complex article or two. Each of these activities demanded a different type of reading skill. Let's take, for example, the way in which we might read a newspaper. Perhaps we'd begin with the headlines. Headlines often force us to read carefully; they include only the barest essentials, so we have to read every word to make sense of them. The information given is so sparse that sometimes we have to read headlines two or three times to get the intended meaning from the words provided. Once we have located a headline which promises an interesting article we may read through the article quickly. Usually when we read like this we are reading basically for the main idea of the passage. If we were asked detailed questions about it, we would have to go back to the article to find the answers. Next we might check the weather report to see what the temperature is going to be, or look up the sports results to see how our favorite team did in its last game. Now we make no attempt to read every word in the article — instead we slide our eyes over the passage looking for the specific piece of information of interest to us.

When we come down to reading individual words, we follow a very similar practice. Our eyes do not read every letter in a word before we identify the word, any more than we read every word in an article before we identify the main point the author is making. Instead our brains in effect make their own headlines. They select only those crucial features of a word or a phrase which we need in order to recognize the meaning. This can be demonstrated very easily. If we are given a very brief glance at a string of random letters such as these

> f z g i h r c t u w d h

we can only identify five or six letters at a time. If the letters are arranged in words, however, as in this example,

> **yet paper snow drive yacht when through**

the same brief glance will enable us to read at least twice as many letters. If the words make a meaningful sentence we can often identify as many as twenty or thirty letters at a glance.

The child was riding a yellow bicycle

If it had to process each letter individually, the brain simply could not process information quickly enough for good readers to read at the speed they do. Instead the brain recognizes chunks of material and processes these chunks rather than individual letters. Exactly the same process applies when we try to remember what we've read. The brain can only hold six or seven items in short term memory. If we try to put too much information into our short-term memory, we push out other items. Let's say we have looked up the phone number 682-7349. We go to the phone muttering 682-7349 and can hold this number fairly well. Suddenly the operator comes on the line and says that the exchange has been changed to 884. By the time we have absorbed this new piece of information, we have forgotten the original number and have to look it up again. The same thing happens with reading. If the brain had to process letter by letter, by the time we got to the end of long words we would have forgotten the beginning. It should be apparent, therefore, that fluent readers are not reading every letter in the words they see, and yet most of us were taught to read by the phonics approach — that is, a process of sounding out each letter in the word. The word **cat** is made up of **cuh-a-tuh**, we were told. Of course it isn't — no child says she saw a black **cuhatuh**. Claiming that **c** gives the sound **cuh** is meaningless. If you know how to pronounce **cat** in the first place, you might be able to work backwards to **cuhatuh** but giving these kinds of rules to students to help them break down new words is not as helpful as we could wish. This is not to say that phonics — decoding letters into sounds — is not of use in learning to read. It does play a part, and it can be a very useful tool, but it should not be the only route or even the primary route we choose.

How do good readers read, then, if they do not rely on phonic skills to break down the words? First of all, we do not come to a piece of print with a completely open mind. The actual format of the print gives us a number of clues which enable us to make a guess at the probable

content, based on our experience. We expect to read something different on the back of a packet of cake-mix from what we read in the newspaper. Illustrations may give us more clues as to the probable content of the material; a text full of numbers gives us different expectations from one with letters. In other words we begin reading with a fair idea of what we will find. We have already ruled out many possibilities simply by observing the way in which the material is presented. We have formulated our first guesses as to the likely content of the material.

When we actually begin to read we continue this process of making educated guesses and reading just enough to confirm or negate our predictions. There are three sources of information available to us. First, we have the actual letters on the page — the orthographic information. As our brain processes the letters in words it is helped tremendously by knowing not only which letters are to be expected but also which letters cannot possibly appear. If the brain recognizes the first letter of a word as **b**, it knows that, in English, the next letter cannot possibly be **c** or **d** or **f** or **g** or many others — in fact there are only eight possible letters that can come after **b** at the beginning of an English word. The further we get into the word, the smaller the number of letters that can follow, and the easier it is for the brain to recognize quickly what the word must be. Therefore, we read fluently, we guess at what a word is likely to be and read only enough letters to confirm our guess.

Secondly there is the order of the words in the sentence — the syntactic information. Because English has set patterns of words that are acceptable, you can probably derive a fair amount of sense from the following passage, even though most of the words will be new to you.

Marlup
A marlup was poving his kump. Parmily a narg horped some whev in his kump. "Why did vump horp whev in my frinkle kump?" the marlup jufd the narg. "Er'm muvvily trungy," the narg grupped. "Er heshed vump horpled whev in your kump. Do vump pove your kump frinkle?"[1]

If you were asked what the **narg horped** in the **marlup's kump**, you would find it fairly easy to answer **whev**, and your answer would be based on the syntax or word order of the sentence. When we are reading material in more familiar language, we can identify in advance what kind of words are likely to arrive. We know that after the word "the" we will read a noun, an adjective, or an adverb, and our predictions as to the likely word will ignore verbs, conjunctions, and articles.

The third and in many ways most important source of information available to us is semantic — the actual meaning of the words. If we are reading an article on gardening, we expect words like **plant, soil,** and **cultivate** but not **plane, boil,** and **calibrate**. We can make logical predictions based on the content of the text, and we don't have to read every letter to distinguish **plant** from **plane**.

Good Readers vs. Poor Readers

Good readers, then, come to the text with certain expectations. They make use of information from three sources — the letters on the page, the word order, and the meaning. They go through the text rapidly, making educated guesses as to the likely content as they go, reading just enough to confirm their predictions. Sometimes, of course, they will predict inaccurately. They may guess **home** for **house** and read on, not even noticing their mistake since it didn't affect the meaning. Sometimes their predictions will lead to nonsense and they will have to go back in the text for further information. What they *don't* do is attempt to read word by word. Thus their short-term memory is never overloaded and they don't find that they have forgotten the beginning of a sentence by the time they reach the end. Poor readers, by contrast, tend to rely heavily on the spelling of words as their major source of

1. Carolyn L. Burke, "The Language Process: Systems or Systematic?" In Richard K. Hodges and E. Hugh Rudorf (eds.), *Language and Learning to Read: What Teachers Should Know about Language*. Boston: Houghton Mifflin, 1972.

information. They read each word and may even struggle from letter to letter, trying to make the word out. They are so occupied with the task of decoding words that they cannot concentrate on meaning, and frequently they have lost the thread of the sentence before they get to the end.

When good and poor readers are asked to read aloud, they illustrate this difference well. Good readers make a surprisingly large number of "errors" in the sense that what they read is not exactly what is in the text. These errors, or *miscues* as they are called, often consist of slight paraphrasings of the text rather than nonsense mistakes. Having misread a present tense as a past tense for instance, they will continue using the past tense so that the material is grammatically sound.

In contrast, poor readers may make fewer miscues, devoting much more attention to the written word, but the errors they make are more significant, changing the meaning of the text or reducing it to nonsense. This is the real difference. Good readers read for the meaning of the text, not for the individual words. Poor readers are so busy struggling with the actual words they have little chance to get the meaning. Current research into reading indicates that we should encourage our students to read for the meaning of the text, not devote their energies to perfect word by word decoding.

READING THEORY AND THE ADULT
SECOND-LANGUAGE LEARNER

As we have seen in the section on Reading Theory, a fluent reader, reading in his/her native language, makes use of information from three areas — spelling, word order, and meaning — in addition to bringing certain expectations to the text based on experience.

It is clear, however, that adult second language (L2) learners are not able to make use of these various information bands as easily as the native language (L1) speaker. To begin with, they may not be able to make predictions as to the likely content of a text based on format if they have no previous experience with literacy or if literacy conventions are different in their native country. They may find the TV listings similar to the sports results, or they may expect all illustrated magazines to contain articles on fashion and beauty.

When L2 learners come to attack the actual print, their limited knowledge of English will obviously make matters more difficult for them. Whereas a native speaker can easily guess the meaning of one unknown word in the context of a sentence, second-language learners are likely to be faced with a number of new vocabulary items and a host of unknown possibilities for every strange word.

L2 learners are likely, too, to have trouble with English syntax, so that word order will not give them the kind of help that it gives native speakers. When unable to predict even which kind of word will come next, they are going to require more information about a word before they can identify it, and they are less likely to be aware of their errors.

L2 literacy students therefore tend to rely very heavily on orthographic information — the actual spelling of the words. Since they have difficulties with predicting, they are likely to attempt to sound out or decode each and every word, and consequently they are subject to problems of short-term memory overload. In their focus on sounding out words, they severely limit their ability to get meaning from the test. If we teach second-language literacy learners exclusively by phonics, we will strongly reinforce this focus. It is important, therefore, that we enable them to make use of other reading strategies which allow them to read for meaning, as a fluent reader does.

As we consider the specific problems of the second-language adult literacy student, we will see differences between the learner who is literate in another language and the learner who is not literate at all. L2 learners who can read in their own language begin with certain advantages. They are trained in the visual discrimination of significant features in letter discrimination. They understand the concept of a particular sound being represented by a particular symbol. They have expectations of a certain content being presented in certain formats. Most important of all, they expect print to yield meaning. This may sound so self-evident as not to be worth mentioning, but it is not unheard of for non-literate students to assume that reading simply means decoding symbols into sounds. Literate students also have a number of word-attack skills. They know that the surrounding context of a word will often give information as to its meaning, and if their native language uses an alphabetic system they will know that breaking a new word down into syllables can make the task of decoding easier.

We would expect, therefore, that students who are literate in one language will already have all the various reading strategies at their fingertips. In practice, however, it appears that even good L1 readers will fail to make use of these strategies if they are faced with an L2 text which is too difficult for them, and they will revert to what we can call the poor-reader strategy of reading word by word because they cannot predict the vocabulary or syntax. It is thus important that the task text should be challenging but not overwhelmingly difficult, and that all students are urged to read for meaning, not just the non-literate ones.

For students approaching literacy for the first time, there are some obvious special needs. They may require training in the pre-reading skills of shape recognition and discrimination. They may have no concept of left-right orientation, and they do not have the concept of sound-symbol correspondence. They may not know what a word is.

Adult students who have never been exposed to print are less likely to have the poor self-image often found in English-speaking illiterates, but students who have had unsuccessful experiences with literacy in their own language often doubt their ability to learn to read, and require special motivation.

Whatever the degree of previous literacy, we can expect some interference from the sound system of the native language. For example students who have great difficulty discriminating between the /i/ sound in **bit** and the /iy/ sound in **beet** are likely to have problems when faced with words in print containing these sounds. Seeing the word **grin** they are likely not just to pronounce it as **green** but to understand it as **green**. Exercises which encourage students to consider the meaning of the text, not merely what it sounds like, are obviously needed here. Listening exercises to encourage sound discrimination are also helpful.

To sum up then, all L2 learners are attempting the reading process without the background language knowledge of the native-speaking learner. Thus prediction, the basis of fluent reading, is that much harder. The best way to offset this is initially to provide texts in which the syntax and the vocabulary are largely familiar, something easily provided if we use the students' speech as the basis for reading material. As students make progress in extracting meaning from the text, we can then incorporate more new items and encourage students to use the familiar context to help them identify new words.

WRITING THEORY

When we talk about someone being able to write, we may be referring to one of two different skills. "He can write very well" referring to 7-year-old Johnny implies that Johnny has the ability to *encode* speech, that is to produce the correct printed symbols to represent the sounds. Said of an adult, however, "He can write very well" implies the ability to express ideas coherently in print, to arrange thoughts logically, and to produce a clear argument. This second type of writing, *cognitive writing*, might well be the eventual aim of our students, and writing exercises which encourage students to think and make judgments about their writing can be usefully included even in fairly elementary ESL classes. However, in this book we will be focussing on the earlier form of writing, the encoding process.

In the early stages of learning to write, the students' attention is devoted almost entirely to the production side of the process, and there is little brain power to spare for the task of critically analysing the content of what they produce. Think of all the demands made on new writers. Even assuming that they know what they want to say when they begin, they must then cope with letter formation, spelling, word order, punctuation, capitalization and possibly even paragraphing. As students get more practice in coping with these demands, they find the process easier and gradually are able to concentrate more on improving the content of what they write, at which point they are probably ready for a regular ESL class.

How do we get students to this point? Basically it is a matter of writing practice combined with reading. The more our students write, the easier they will find the process. In effect, the brain is learning new habits. When we first learn to drive a car, we feel called upon to do six different things at once, and yet after a little experience we find that we can perform the required tasks in sequence without any conscious thought. Similarly when we are writing, our brains don't instruct our fingers to produce one letter after another in sequence. There simply wouldn't be time for the messages to travel down our arms to our fingers if the brain waited for one letter to be finished before it sent the signals to start the next letter. Instead the brain learns whole patterns of movements and is already sending messages to the fingers to produce the second and third letter of a word when the pen is tracing out the first letter. By frequent writing we train our brain to work in these sequences, just as we trained it (for example) to cope with the various actions involved in moving out to overtake another car.

If writing improves with practice, then where does reading come in? Reading helps us recognize acceptable word patterns and acceptable spellings. Many of us, when asked how to spell a word, will check it in print to see if it "looks right." The brain has learned, from frequent reading, which combination of letters make up a particular word, just as we know which combination of features make up a friend's face — even though we might have trouble describing it.

Writing is often considered to be a more difficult task than reading. The writer has to make use of the same conventions of letter order, word order, and meaning as the reader does, but because writing is a productive skill the demands made on the individual are more strict. Many of us could understand a sentence pattern in a foreign language which, however, we could not produce. We often have no trouble reading words which we cannot spell. In some ways though, writing can be a simpler process than reading, speaking, or listening. Struggling to write in a second language, we can avoid difficult constructions, find alternatives for unknown vocabulary, and generally choose our own route based on our capabilities in the language. Unlike reading, where the content may be a mystery to us, in writing we control the content. Also we can make as many attempts at the writing process as we need

to achieve a finished product which satisfies us. While we are still having problems with content we don't need to worry about spelling, perfect grammar, or legibility. All these can be incorporated into later drafts or into a final tidy copy. Students often find this idea of a rough draft and a fair copy very appealing, as it enables them to attempt something challenging but still end up with a piece of writing of which they can be proud.

WRITING THEORY AND THE ADULT SECOND-LANGUAGE LEARNER

When native speakers first learn to write they normally devote all their attention to the simple task of getting the letters right. Even a small child has a firm grasp of sentence structure and a wide vocabulary to call on, so that concentration can be focussed on the demands of spelling and legibility. For the second-language learner, however, the demands are much greater. Whereabouts in the sentence should the verb come, and what tense should be used? What's the English word for that action anyway? The L2 learner is struggling for control of all the different aspects of writing at once, aggravated by the adult mentality which wants to produce something meaningful, not just the repetition of simple phrases.

As in learning to read, students who are literate in their native language have writing skills which can help them in English. They know how to hold a pen correctly and they have the fine muscle control necessary for legible handwriting. They understand the concept of a word and recognize word boundaries. Their own language may be written in a different direction from English (right to left and/or in vertical rather than horizontal lines) but they expect a consistent pattern of direction and usually find it easy to change to left-right directionality. The learner who is not literate in any language is unlikely to have any of these skills and will accordingly need more practice.

Many second-language students have difficulty distinguishing certain sounds. They may hear no difference between /b/ and /v/, for instance. When they come to write words containing these sounds they have no way of judging from the sound of the word which letters are required. While it is possible for them to learn new words, which include the difficult sound, on a letter-by-letter basis, this is a very time-consuming process and does not help them attack other new words. If the teacher can do work on listening to help them distinguish the appropriate sounds, the students will find spelling an easier process.

Spelling is also a matter of knowing the acceptable patterns of letters in the language. When native speakers attempt to write a new word, they know that certain patterns such as **qm** are never used in English, and restrict their choices accordingly. Second-language students have to learn what combinations of letters and sounds are permissible in English. They may be able to use **nf** to start a word in their language, but it is never an acceptable combination at the start of an English word, despite the fact that they will frequently hear ''hamburger 'n'fries please''. This kind of knowledge is not something that can be usefully taught in a formal way, but will develop from exposure to printed English.

The limited English vocabularies of second-language learners also slow their progress. Native speakers can learn whole groups of words which share common features — having conquered the silent **gh** spelling conventions, they have a tool to attack **right, sight, fight, light,** and **might**. Second-language learners may not have these words in their vocabulary, so that it is less easy for them to generalize.

Most of all, second-language learners are hindered by their lack of control of syntax or grammar. Strange constructions that work quite adequately for them in speech, supported by intonation, facial expression, and gesture, can be incomprehensible in the baldness of print. Students need to learn the basic structural patterns of English and develop a sense of what constitutes a sentence.

It is obvious, therefore, that even in a class devoted exclusively to literacy there is a place for oral language work. If the students are to spell correctly they will need listening exercises to ensure that they hear words properly. If they are to form adequate sentences they will need speech work to try out sentence patterns and develop vocabulary. Whether focussing primarily on reading or writing, we will achieve greater success in the early stages if the print reflects language with which the students are orally familiar.

3 / Particular Factors to Bear in Mind in the Adult Class

Before we examine the differences between children and adults as learners, it should of course be stressed that in many ways good teaching methodology is the same for all age groups. All learners do better when the teaching is cooperative and students can share in the process of information exchange, rather than when the learning is passive and teacher-directed. Giving our students the opportunity to share their knowledge and experience makes the learning both more pleasant and more effective. It is important that our students contribute to our classes and play an active role, not just in activities we have designed, but in contributing ideas, solving each other's problems, and teaching us.

Although in general terms this approach is valid for both children and adults, there are areas where adult students have special abilities that we can capitalize on, and special needs to be met.

Life Experience

One of the most important differences is the storehouse of experience the adult possesses. All adult ESL students have proved themselves able to survive in at least two different cultures. Many are far more travelled than their teachers are. They have learned to judge people, think independently, and weigh facts critically. It is important not to forget these abilities even though the students cannot express them verbally in English. Adult students are far more likely to question our teaching than children are, and they need the opportunity to do so.

Self-Image

Adult students may feel that school is an inappropriate place for persons of their age. They will therefore be particularly sensitive to anything

that seems to imply that the teacher regards them as children. This is
not just a matter of avoiding talking down to students, or not using
children's primers. It is much more a matter of giving students responsibility for their own learning. Let them choose the topic or approach.
If they feel unhappy working in small groups and prefer to work alone,
give them that choice. Don't fall into the trap of simplifying content
in an attempt to simplify language. Make suggestions rather than give
orders. Allow the students to demonstrate their adult skills and abilities,
and let them teach you. Don't play the infallible teacher. If you can
admit your mistakes, the students won't feel so foolish when they make
mistakes too.

Physical Factors

There are a number of physical factors to be borne in mind in the adult
classroom. The most obvious is simply the size of an adult. Too often
classes held in school facilities involve squeezing six-foot adults into

desks designed for three-foot children. Often the solution can be as simple as requesting the use of the staff room during evening hours, or bringing in chairs from the auditorium. Reading and writing is a sufficient challenge without being physically cramped in the process.

Another physical factor to bear in mind is the possibility of older students having poor hearing or eyesight. As well as making sure that students know how to go about gettting any treatment necessary, we need to provide seating arrangements flexible enough to allow such students to choose seats close to the teacher, blackboard, or tape recorder.

A third factor is fatigue. Many of our students carry a heavy workload in addition to attending classes, and their powers of concentration are likely to be diminished. Variety in classroom activities, opportunities to move around and stretch, and the inevitable stand-by of a kettle and a jar of instant coffee all help to combat their fatique.

Nature of the Contract Between Teacher and Student

In our society the occupation allocated to children is primarily that of student. Not only *must* they attend school, but the contract runs for a number of years. The teacher can therefore count on having a certain length of time for study patterns to reach fruition.

The nature of the contract with the adult student is very different. For most adults, studying is not their primary role — it is something they have to fit in around the demands of their jobs and families. Normally it is the activity most easily sacrificed when conflicting demands are made on their time. Attendance is voluntary — students can skip classes or drop out entirely if the classes don't fulfil their expectations.

Making our lessons interesting and useful is obviously the first step to encouraging regular attendance, but we probably have to expect that some students will miss classes occasionally because of other commitments. This makes it difficult to have each lesson build on the previous one — a problem aggravated by continuous intake of students. Some of the techniques we can use to overcome the problem are group work, frequent review, individualized tasks, and recycling of material previously covered by placing it in a fresh context.

The length of the contract is another major difference in adult ESL instruction. Few adult students can spare the time to learn the theoretical principles first and the application later, even if they really felt that this would improve their competence in the long run. Rather they are looking for a quick return on their investment of time and energy, and want lesson content which they can take out into the street and use immediately. This of course is the reason that such stress is laid on planning lessons around the students' needs.

Students' Expectations of the Teacher

In a single class an ESL teacher is likely to be faced with a variety of learning styles. One student will sit rigidly at attention and want to repeat each word after the teacher. Another will expect to demonstrate prowess by challenging the teacher at every turn. A third may only feel happy with the security of a workbook to be worked through diligently, while a fourth may have no study skills at all and find it extremely difficult to maintain concentration. A fifth may learn everything by rote, yet have no understanding of meaning.

It is impossible to adopt a teaching style which pleases everyone all the time, yet it is necessary for the teacher to be prepared to modify the approach if this makes the students feel more at ease. We might not feel that there is a suitable workbook we want to use, but we can satisfy the students who work this way by providing a folder of worksheets we have prepared ourselves. If some students are very ill at ease with group discussions, for the first few weeks they could work individually on a task. Most teachers find that students are prepared to adapt to new teaching styles if the transition is made gently, not abruptly.

4 / Content of ESL Literacy Lessons

BASIC PARAMETERS IN LESSON PLANNING

Although literacy students come from disparate backgrounds and have different needs, there are some basic parameters which can help us plan classes for second-language learners. The first of these parameters is the importance of oral work. Whether for reading or for writing, ESL students have to develop their vocabulary and their control of sentence patterns. For the reading side, they need to expand these skills to enable them to improve their prediction abilities, and for the writing side to permit them to concentrate on the physical process of forming letters and words. It is not just a matter of doing oral work in the regular ESL class and then waiting for the benefits to become apparent in the literacy sessions, although this will happen. It also involves using oral language as the springboard for literacy activities. The class can talk about the probable content of a reading passage before students attempt to read it. Stories dictated by the students and written down by the teacher can be used as reading texts. Writing will be easier if the students have first grappled with the topic orally, trying out new vocabulary and structures. When the content of the reading or writing is familiar, the students have a much greater chance of success, and their attention can be focussed on the meaningful reading or writing process, rather than on the limitations of their language competence.

The second point to bear in mind is that there is no automatic entry point for learning to read and write. One doesn't have to begin with three-letter words like **cat** and **dog**, when adults will obviously be more interested in the words they see on street signs or the names of the subway stations. Reading and writing can begin with any words, even if at first sight the words our students want to learn seem complicated in their spelling. Many of the common short words, such as **my, said,**.

and **right** are irregular phonetically, and yet small children are expected to master them easily in their basal primers.

The point of entry for our adult students should be their areas of interest and need. Reading material which students perceive as meaningful improves motivation and breeds success. As we have stated earlier, adult students come to literacy classes for many reasons, but often they will have a particular aim in mind: to get their driver's license, to be able to write down phone messages at work, or to read their children's school reports, for example. If we begin the reading and writing process using materials based on students' needs, we will find that their high level of interest and motivation make the task much easier. Rather than conquering the reading and writing of sentences such as **See Nan in the tan van**, which will be of little immediate use to them, learning to write a cheque or read the labels on generic supermarket products gives them a demonstrable sign of their progress and a skill which they can usefully employ outside the classroom.

Related to this point of teaching to our students' needs is the importance of **using material suitable for adults**. Most of the commonly available material specifically produced for teaching literacy is intended for children, and is likely to be offensive to mature adults. Only when adults specifically state that they want to be able to read stories to their children should children's picture books be used. There are many other materials available with limited vocabulary which are of much greater interest to adults. Short forms such as bank slips, for example, make few demands of word order or punctuation and can be found or made up with a minimum of vocabulary. Advertising flyers follow a similar format; catalogues are as lavishly illustrated as any children's book and give the same amount of context clues. It is important that our adult students do not feel they are being treated as children, but that we respect their more varied interests and acknowledge their wider experience.

Some of the other basic issues in the teaching of adult literacy, regardless of the specific approach used, are less clear cut. One such issue is the question of whether students should begin writing simultaneously with reading, or whether it is better to develop their reading skills a little prior to beginning writing. People have been taught successfully by both methods and each method appears to have advantages. Proponents of reading first claim that students do a better job of letter reproduction when they have enough reading experience to recognize which features of a letter are significant. For example, we recognize the letter **t** whether we see it written straight up and down or slanted, with or without the curl at the bottom of the down stroke. We know the significant features are the long down stroke and the short cross stroke approximately one-third of the way down. Students new

to literacy have no way of knowing this if the first **t** they see, is in a type face which has wiggly ends to all the strokes. Only by exposure to numerous **t**'s can they begin to recognize the crucial features which distinguish **t** from all other letters. An example of this confusion over essential features is illustrated in this form completed by a new literacy student who has painstakingly reproduced the type-written characters on her visa. (See p. 26.)

Other teachers, however, claim that students learn to distinguish these significant features more rapidly when they are called upon to write them themselves. To some extent the question of reading first or reading and writing together will be answered by the demands of the students. Students who are already literate in the native language will probably express a wish to write from the first lesson. Other students may prefer to gain some competence in reading and are happy to postpone the writing process. Listen to what your students tell you and choose accordingly.

A similar issue is the choice of script in which to begin writing, and again there are arguments on both sides. Teaching adults manuscript printing to begin allows them in their reading and their writing to use a single set of symbols, and is not too demanding in the early days. However, some adults see printing in manuscript as childish, and feel strongly that they wish to learn cursive writing. Teachers may wish to begin immediately with cursive, therefore, and not waste time on

26

YANG

A23-744-398| 06 8-57-4 2|

NAME YANG KAN/ MY NAME IS /CA94 10

Last First Name

IAOS

ADDRESS (IRC)12 4 645 BUSH ST. H 307 |127|

ICEM Number Street Apt. #

SAN FRANCIS SW CA 9410 8

(IRC)127 City State Zip Code 4760

TELEPHONE NUMBER Phon@e messag 98 2 AGE 36

MY SCHOOL Sgt 11 Wg116t St

PLACE OF BIRTH BIRTHDATE 7-20-1942

XIENG KHOUANG IAOS |SF / VISAS EALCON-

JULY 20-1942

Write the answer:

1. What day is today? GDFhCr OJMARKE F |12 JULY 1978

2. What is today's date? _____

3. Where are you from? Montgomery st san Efrancisco CA 94101

4. Where do you live? _____

5. What are you doing now? _____

6. How old are you? _____

7. How are you? _____

8. What is your name? _____

9. What is your birthdate? _____

10. What color is your shirt? _____

THE IGNACT To

Indefite

Idotidhkefu

Write the question: purpose

1. _____ . I am from New York.

2. _____ . I am 37 years old.

3. _____ . My shirt is blue.

4. _____ . I live in San Francisco.

5. _____ . Fine. thanks.

Month, Day and year Visa issued potre

(kgh yahg)(YONG XIONG) 0685 79 2 OAI(III)IPP 2°

(XAY XIONG)-(VALEE XIONG) EMP Ioyment AuthoT

LoS-277-SEP-08 78

the intermediate stage of printing. Again this is a question which we can usually resolve by identifying the wishes and needs of the students. Manuscript printing is called for on many forms and indeed numerous literate adults commonly use printing, so that unless the students express a real preference for cursive writing it is probably easier to start students with manuscript. Teachers who use this method claim that the transition to cursive proceeds smoothly when it is presented as the mere joining of manuscript letters. Even with students who want cursive initially, there seems little point in teaching cursive capitals. Native speakers increasingly use block letters not only for completing forms but also as part of their cursive system, as in this example.

John Forsyth,
16 St. Georges Avenue,
Torville, Quebec.

In sum, therefore, the type of letters we choose to teach first will reflect the types of things our students want to read and write. The worker who does not want to seem illiterate on the job will want to learn cursive. The young adult trying the driving test will want to read print and write block letters. If our class is composed of students with a wide variety of needs, we will probably begin with print lerrers as the system most commonly encountered.

DEFINING THE NEEDS OF THE LEARNER

Because motivation is such a crucial feature in the progress of the adult literacy student, teachers need to plan their lessons carefully to make sure that what they teach is relevant to their students' needs. This is particularly true for teaching content. Too often we think of reading as reading a book, and yet most of us use our reading skills far more frequently for such things as menus, street signs, bank statements, pay slips, calendars, TV listings, and the like. These are the kinds of things our adult students are likely to want to read, not great literature. This isn't to say that our literacy students shouldn't be introduced to the idea of reading for pleasure rather than just reading for information, but in the early stages they will need successful feedback of literacy skills which help them in their everyday life. Once the mechanics of reading become less of an effort, they will enjoy reading for pleasure much more. In

the meantime, the concept of interest reading can be introduced by the teacher reading to the students. Short articles from the newspaper or *Reader's Digest*, comics and photo romances, cartoons, perhaps a write-up of a favorite sports team's most recent performance, or even a short poem can be usefully read to the class. As the class progresses, these readings may become the basis for oral discussion, and the students may want to create simplified versions as reading or writing exercises. In the very earliest classes, however, the students are likely to be most motivated to tackle materials, such as food labels, which frustrate them in everyday life.

Identifying our students' needs is not always easy if the class has too limited a command of English to volunteer information for themselves, and if interpreters are not available. We can often make some educated guesses, however, based on what we know of the class. Students with school-aged children are likely to feel a need for help with the letters sent home from school, and the associated demand for writing permission slips or notes to the teacher. The students' occupations may give us a clue — cleaners probably need to write notes regarding supplies which need replacing, mechanics may need to jot down phone messages regarding cars coming into the garage. Unemployed workers or people on Workmen's Compensation may need help filling out their claim forms, and anyone paid by cheque will want help with banking procedure.

An easy way of encouraging students to indicate their areas of need and interest is to build up a reading file from which students pick out items that they would like to read. Such a box might contain a variety of forms, photographs of street signs, illustrated newspaper articles, excerpts from the want ads, food packages, recipes, short stories and articles on a wide range of subjects, cartoons, maps, medicine labels, comic strips, schedules, instructions, pamphlets, and menus. Wherever possible such items should have illustrations, or a format which provides a clue to the content.

Any of the items in such a reading file would be a valid and valuable place to begin reading. To accompany such activities, however, we need material which draws on the students' own interests and experiences and acknowledges the storehouse of experience which the adult possesses. Adults learn more effectively when the learning is cooperative, when they can share in the process of information exchanging, rather than when the learning is passive and teacher-directed. As we have pointed out before, giving our students the opportunity to share their knowledge and experience makes the learning more pleasant and more effective. It is important, then, that our students contribute to our classes and play an active role. How do we manage to achieve this in the classroom, given the confines of the limited time schedule, the language problems, and the varied interests?

Partly it is a matter of being flexible with our lesson planning so that issues of interest raised by the students can be adequately explored. It also involves encouraging students to open up to the class, whether by demonstrating a special skill such as woodwork, or sharing a problem such as the assembly of a child's bike, or finding a new apartment. Often a concrete item, such as photographs of the students as children, will encourage students to offer accounts of their own related experiences. Stories told by the students and written down by the teacher will make excellent reading practice and can also be the basis for written work. Above all it is a matter of making reading writing activities not only out of the students' urgent needs but also out of their interests and experiences.

SKILLS REQUIRED IN READING

Before we can decide how we are going to teach our students literacy, we need to clarify exactly what it is we want them to learn. Although experts have defined long lists of skills employed by the fluent reader (as many as 200), we can usefully concentrate on two major groups: first, the skills which help us decode printed symbols into words, and second, the skills which help up get meaning from a written or printed text. There is some overlap between these categories, and information which helps us decode a word will often help us recognize the meaning too.

Decoding Skills

a. Pre-Reading Skills

To read in English we need to understand that English is normally written from left to right and from top to bottom. We need also to be able to discriminate sufficiently between small shapes so that we can distinguish the curve of a **u** from the straight line of a **v**, or the left-facing **d** from the right-facing **b**. To illustrate how difficult this can be in a strange script, try the following exercise using Japanese characters.

1) Identify the character which is the same as the one in the box at the left.
2) One character is reversed. Which one?
3) Copy the character in the box at the left. What problems do you face?

b. Phonic Skills

We need to recognize the letters and have some understanding of the various sounds which each letter can represent, either alone or in combination with other letters. We need familiarity with such combinations of letters to recognize which ones are possible and whereabouts in a word they are likely to occur. If we know that **tm** is not a permissible combination within a syllable, for instance, we won't attempt to decode postmaster as **pos-tma-ster**. (For a list of common English syllables, see Appendix B.)

c. Vocabulary.

Because English spelling does not always tell us the pronunciation of a word, we need a reasonable oral vocabulary so that our decoding in terms of possible words enables us to recognize the right word when we have it.

d. Word Attack Skills.

If we are faced with a word which gives us problems, there are a number of strategies which help with decoding. For instance, we might break down a word like **difficult** into syllables. We might decode a word like **night** by recognizing its similarity to a known work like **fight**. We can recognize compound words like **fireplace** as being made up of the possibly familiar **fire** and **place**. We can use our knowledge of English suffixes and prefixes to help determine the meaning of the word; for instance, we know the word **misbehaved** has something to do with **behave**. We can use our knowledge of sentence patterns to determine what kind of word we are dealing with, so that we expect the letters **ing** to form part of a verb, for example.

All these skills will help us make out the actual words which the printed letters signify. Also there will be **sight words**, words which we recognize by their particular shape or format, just as a small child recognizes the word **McDonald's** without any attempt to decode it letter by letter.

While skills of identifying words are by no means all there is to reading, they are the skills on which comprehension is built. Before we can read for meaning we have to be able to identify a fair number of words in the text, whether we recognize them on sight, or decipher them by identifying their individual letters or groups of letters. When we have reached this point we can employ the various strategies which enable us to understand the text.

Comprehension Skills

a.   Using Context Clues

Getting the meaning from a piece of text is greatly simplified if we capitalize on the information which the context gives us. As mentioned earlier, the format of the text gives us information. We can all recognize the difference between a recipe and a bus schedule without reading a word. Location of the item on a page also helps us; for example, the words above the signature on a business letter will probably be some form of closing off remark.

Within the sentence, the *context* helps us to get the meaning of unknown words or phrases. If we read **"It was a really stormy night and the wind was _____ "** we can be pretty sure that the missing word must be something like **howling**. Our knowledge of sentence structure tells us it can't be a word like **rain** and our understanding of the meaning of key words like **wind** and **stormy** tells us it can't be **writing** or **pretty**.

Certain vocabulary items will also give us clues. Words such as **first, then,** and **finally** warn us that various steps in a procedure or argument are forthcoming. **However** or **nevertheless** warn us that the next statement will be in contrast to what we have just read.

b. Skimming

Skimming involves reading over a text very quickly to get a general idea of what the writer is trying to say. It does not involve reading each and every word, but rather looking for the key words which give the meaning. It is the kind of reading we do when we glance at the newspaper or browse through books in the library to decide what we want to borrow. Skimming a text quickly gives us a good idea of the content and facilitates any more careful reading which we may want to do later, since we can now predict much more accurately based on our knowledge of the text.

c. Scanning

Scanning is the procedure we follow when we want to locate a specific item of information in a text. We slide our eyes over the entire text looking for particular key words. For instance, we might want or order a hamburger for lunch, and scan the menu quickly to see if hamburgers are offered and if so at what price. In doing this we are not reading all the words until we come to the word **hamburger**. Rather we are identifying these other words simply as *not hamburger* — a much quicker

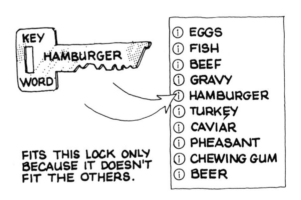

process. Think of how rapidly we can run through a list of names in a phonebook looking for the one particular name of interest to us.

d. Reading for Thorough Understanding

This is the kind of detailed reading that is commonly taught in schools. It does have a value, but it should be borne in mind that adults frequently don't need to read material in such depth. Reading for thorough understanding involves recognizing the main idea, recognizing the supporting details, appreciating such things as cause and effect, and tone and mood, so that, for instance, a satire is not taken seriously.

For the L2 students, added onto all these reading skills is of course the development of language skills. It cannot be stressed enough that development of vocabulary and knowledge of sentence patterns will help students both with decoding and with comprehension, and this side of ESL literacy cannot be forgotten.

SKILLS REQUIRED IN WRITING

Many of the skills we have discussed in reading have their counterparts in the writing process — various skills related to encoding, and skills which improve the content of what we write. The *encoding skills* include pre-writing skills such as pen control, left-right directionality, and fine muscle coordination. As in reading, a knowledge of sound-symbol correspondence assists in spelling, supported by the development of a bank of sight words whose spelling has been learned thoroughly. Vocabularly and sentence structure are obviously demanded, as is at least a minimum of knowledge about punctuation and capitalization.

Improving the content of the writing (for example, by asking students to use topic sentences) is not normally considered part of the literacy task, in that students who have conquered the basics of writing in terms of recording oral language are normally able to cope well in regular ESL classes. While the fine art of rhetoric need not be our concern, the road to good writing is a continuous process, and there is no reason why we cannot help students to take their first steps on this road once they find the encoding process less demanding. For instance, students may reach the point at which they can write a brief account of what they did on the weekend. While they are struggling with the first draft, they need to concentrate on the encoding process. But even before they write, we could discuss the sequence of events so that they come to their writing task with their ideas in order. Before they copy out a finished product, students might read each other's work and see if any crucial information is missing. We might help them focus on the main point of the story by asking them to provide a title. These kinds of activities help students' writing to progress in terms of style without making too many demands simultaneously.

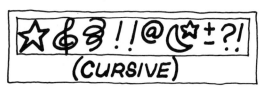
(CURSIVE)

5 / Teaching Pre-Literacy

Literacy teaching has been going on for hundreds of years, and not surprisingly therefore there are many different approaches, ranging from memorizing large chunks of the Koran to color-coding alphabets (each sound having a different color). On the whole, though, the approaches fall into one of two patterns; either they concentrate initially on the decoding aspect of the process, or they concentrate initially on the comprehension aspect. Both these types of approach presuppose the development of pre-literacy skills.

PRE-LITERACY SKILLS

a) Pre-Reading Skills

Reading readiness in children is usually considered in terms of their maturity and their command of oral language. Adults obviously have fulfilled the demands of maturity and, while they may lack competence in English, have complete command of their native language and thus have an understanding of how language operates. They may not, however, have had any need to develop their ability to discriminate between small shapes, or to recognize common features in groups of objects. They may lack the fine muscle coordination necessary to wield a pen, and in older students problems can be aggravated by poor sight, poor hearing, and such things as arthritis.

It may be necessary therefore to provide pre-reading activities with students, particularly those who have no previous literacy experience. Because such tasks can seem demeaning to adults, it is important that students are allowed to make progress as rapidly as possible, and not held back on exercises which are not challenging to them while the rest of the class catches up.

Pre-reading skills are most likely to be necessary for the completely non-literate student. A student who has spent all his life recognizing that a cow is a cow whether it faces left or right will not instantly appreciate the significance of the difference between **p** and **q** without it being pointed out. Students who are literate in their own language already have training in this regard. If their own language uses the roman alphabet they may need no pre-reading training at all. Students whose native languages do not use the roman alphabet, however, may need practice with such things as direction and letter formation, and could benefit from some of the later exercises in this section. They may need work on visual discrimination of features which are significant in English but not meaningful in their native language, such as the relative size of **S** and **s**.

Some students come from cultures where artwork consists solely of pattern representations and have therefore had little exposure to the idea of representing three-dimensional shapes on a flat surface. A simple line drawing of an apple, for instance, will be perceived merely as a circular shape, not as a symbol of a known fruit. A corollary of this is that they may have great difficulty with such things as maps, as well as the general problem of understanding that written shapes can be symbols of objects or sounds.

The first step in pre-reading skills training is to develop the students' ability to discriminate between shapes. It should not be assumed that a student does not have this ability simply because he or she is non-literate in the first language. Many students are skilled at hobbies and crafts, such as embroidery, which have already developed this skill. Others will find even the first exercises challenging.

Initially shape discrimination should focus on major differences, such as between circles and squares. Later it should focus on features which are significant for letter shapes, such as left- or right-facing characters. It is not advisable to spend time on features such as thick or thin lines which have no significance for letter recognition.

Figure 1 shows some possible components of early shape discrimination exercises in which the student is asked to identify the ''different'' shape.

Asking the student to find a similar shape from a row of different shapes is a slightly harder task (figure 2).

Gradually the exercises become harder as the choice of items increases, the size of items decreases, and the differences become less noticeable (figure 3).

In the final stage of shape discrimination the student is working with actual letters in a normal type face (figure 4).

At this point upper and lower case letters can be introduced, and also numbers.

Student circles different shape.

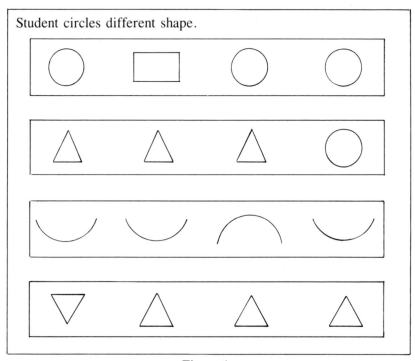

Figure 1

Student circles matching shape.

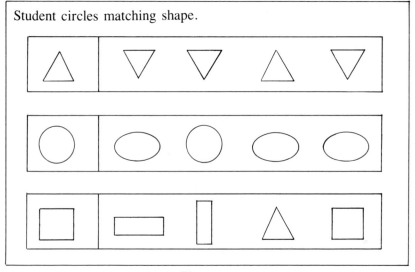

Figure 2

Student circles matching shape.

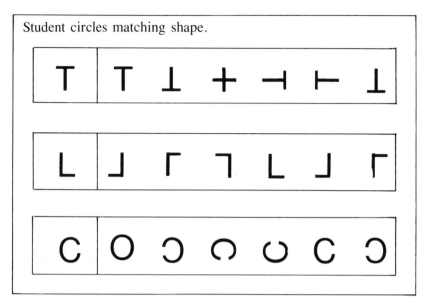

Figure 3

Student circles all the matching shapes.

a   o   e   b   a   c   f   a

p   q   b   d   q   p   t

m   m   n   w   u   u

Figure 4

Such exercises do not formally teach the students what the letters are, but as the eye is trained to recognize significant features of the shapes, the letters and numbers become familiar and are therefore more easily learned.

While working on shape discrimination most teachers simultaneously introduce the written form of personal language such as name, address, and phone number. Following oral work on the lines of "What's your name? My name is _____ ," the teacher writes the word **name** on the blackboard, and points out to the students the word **name** on their discrimination exercises. On the first exercise the teacher writes each student's name on the paper, and on subsequent exercises the student is expected to copy this. Gradually the words **first, last, address,** and so on, are introduced in similar fashion, until the students reach the point where they can complete a brief form such as that shown in figure 5.

Name_____
          FIRST   LAST

Address_____

Telephone Number_____

Figure 5

While the students' first attempts at copying such information are not likely to be very satisfactory, all the students will recognize the value of what they are writing and will feel that they have gained something concrete from the class (which they may not find in shape-discrimination work). Also, the wide variety of letters and numbers likely to be employed in such personal information gives them a chance to recognize letters when they are first introduced as part of the alphabet.

When students come to learn individual letters it is not necessarily advisable to approach the letters in alphabetical order initially. There does not seem to be very clear evidence as to which letters it is best to begin with, although some teachers claim that students experience less confusion if similar letters are presented together and the distinctive features pointed out. The letters **M, N,** and **W** can therefore be taught as a group which share the features of straight lines in upper case, and lines and curves in lower case. One rule which it is wise to follow is not to begin with letters such as **C,** which have more than one sound. When a letter is introduced, it should be presented on the board in upper and lower case and immediatley placed in a word, preferably the name of one of the students. The teacher says something like, "This is the letter **T**. It's the letter which makes the first sound in Tomas. Do you know any other words which begin with the same sound as Tomas?" It is not a good idea to identify the letter as making a **tuh** sound, which is obviously a distortion of the way **T** actually functions in Tomas. Instead, various words beginning with **T** can be used to model the sound. Students can then check their name and address cards to see if the letter **T** appears there, and listen to see if they can hear the sound. A system of index cards can be used to help the memory process. After coming up with a number of words which begin with the chosen sound, students choose one word as their particular memory prop, preferably something which can be easily drawn. They then make a card showing the letter, together with their chosen key word and an illustration as an available reminder of the sound. (See figure 6.) Later, other **t** words can be added to the card and the cards can be arranged in alphabetical order.

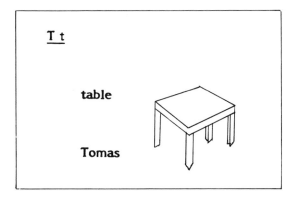

T t

table

Tomas

Figure 6

It is reassuring for students to be aware that there is a finite number of symbols to be learned. A demonstration of the entire alphabet, and the information that every word in English is made up of a combination of some of these 26 letters, is valuable. It should be made clear to students that each letter has only one name but that it may make more than one stound, and that each letter has an upper- and lower-case form. Generally, of course, we do want our students to be familiar with alphabetical order, so they can use such things as dictionaries and telephone directories. Having the alphabet permanently written up across the top of the blackboard is helpful. (Some more detailed suggestions for teaching alphabetical order are included later, in section 10, Other Useful Activities.)

Numbers are somewhat easier to teach as they do not hinge on a particular culture or language. Even though students may not be skilled in arithmetic, nearly all of them will understand the idea of numbers, and simply need to learn the new names and symbols.

Since Arabic numerals are in wider use than the roman alphabet, there will be a number of students who, while faced with a completely new alphabet, will be quite at home with our numbering system. For those to whom Arabic numbers are unknown, it is useful to build up a card file showing the number plus an equivalent number of dots (figure 7).

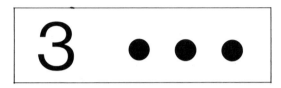

Figure 7

Playing cards are useful tools in teaching numbers, and can be put together in pairs to make double-digit numbers if necessary.

b) Pre-Writing Skills

Much of the work described under Pre-Reading Skills will help the students approach writing. The particular demands of writing are concerned with fine muscle coordination. Many students find letter formation easier if they begin attempting to form the shapes on a large scale. Rather than attempting individual letters at the start, attention should be paid to producing the general type of required movements. Circles progressing from left to right and slanted lines all moving in the same direction are usually the first exercises (see figure 8).

Figure 8

Many teachers find that asking their students to draw such shapes in the air is a satisfactory introduction. There is no possibility of mistake in an air-drawn shape, and the student gains practice in using the entire arm to write, rather than working with the rigid fist seen in some literacy students. Using the blackboard for large-scale drawing is usually the next step, which again encourages students to work for ease and flow, rather than tight control. There is a limit, though, to how much blackboard work adults will tolerate, and it is necessary to watch out for signs of dissatisfaction among the students.

Once the students begin to work with pencil and paper, they may need to be shown how to hold the pencil and how to angle the paper slightly, to allow ease of movement for the arm. Again, some loosening-up exercises (as in fig. 8) will be useful before students progress to letter formation. In the early days there is really little alternative to tracing and copying. Some teachers find that having their students begin by using their fingers to trace the letters on a textured surface such as sandpaper or velvet helps them remember the shapes. The multi-sensory approach is further reinforced if students repeat the name of the letter as they trace it.

When students are copying letters we may see them beginning at what we consider the wrong part of a letter. Some idosyncratic approaches are more significant than others. Getting into the habit of drawing the letter **o** clockwise rather than counter-clockwise really won't make much difference to their eventual writing speed. Consistently drawing an **m** by beginning with the right-hand stroke will cause problems, however. They may not have sufficient space to complete the letter if it is situated in the middle of a word and they will find the transition to cursive extremely difficult if they are constantly working in the wrong direction. Students can build up some sense of the approach to letters if they are aware of the importance of left-right direction within letters as well as within words. For particularly sticky problems we may have to resort to arrows showing the direction of the pen stroke, or numbering strokes in order of performance, as in figure 9. (Occasionally there are problems with this, as students may attempt to copy the arrows and numbers too, not yet being aware of the significant features of the letters. Understanding of what constitutes a given letter will come as the students are exposed to various type faces and to the irregularity of the teacher's printing. This understanding will be reinforced by the students' writing practice and should soon cease to be a problem.)

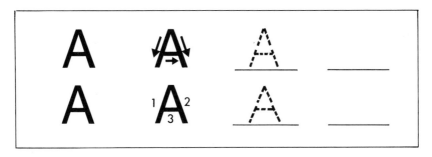

Figure 9

6 / Teaching Reading

When we come to consider ways of actually teaching students to read, it is apparent that we can approach the subject in two ways. We can begin with whole pieces of language which are then broken down into individual words, syllables, and letters. Or we can begin with the individual letters and sounds and build up to the words and sentences. Most of us learned to read by the second method. We learned the sound for **d** and **o** and **g** and worked through **duh-o-guh** to reach **dog**. We approached new words in a similar way by beginning with the most basic elements and building up. It is tempting to conclude that as we all learned to read fluently by this method, it will therefore be a successful method with our students. However, our students are not small children learning in their native language, with years of full-time study ahead of them in which to conquer literacy. Nor do we have any proof that we learned to read in the most efficient way. Perhaps we are fluent readers *despite* having learned by this method. Certainly many failures among the English-speaking population were taught by this method.

Teaching exclusively by phonic analysis puts emphasis on the decoding aspect of reading, and ignores the meaning. While literacy students obviously need to be able to decode words enough to recognize them, we do not want them to form reading habits limited to sounding-out words. It is quite possible to read something aloud fluently without having any understanding of it, as was demonstrated by the Marlup exercise on page 12. Armed with a couple of rules of pronunciation, most of us could do an admirable job of reading a Latin text aloud, but we wouldn't necessarily have any idea of what we were saying. Nor is this situation restricted to reading in an unknown language. We can illustrate this point by imagining Gloria, a Hollywood movie star, who is presented by the studio with a legal contract. Faced with "The party of the first part, hereinafter referred to . . . ", she phones her New York lawyer for advice, and is told, "Read it to me." This she does. The lawyer

then explains the major points to her and suggests the changes she might request. Obviously both partners in this exchange play a part in the reading process. Gloria's sounding-out of the text was of no use without the lawyer's comprehension of the sounds. Both partners *read* this material. Gloria read the sounds. The lawyer read the meaning.

ESL literacy students are often in a position similar to that of the movie star, and they tend to respond in the same way. Gloria was not facing a completely unknown language. Many of the words in the contract were familiar vocabulary to her. Many of the sentence patterns were familiar. She even had some sense of what she expected to find in the contract. And yet, the sprinkling of unknown legal terms, the unusual use of words otherwise familiar, and the occasional unfamiliar sentence structure were enough to make her give up any attempt at understanding the document, beyond sounding it out.

This is what can happen to our ESL literacy students. Faced by new vocabulary, new structures, and an insecure grasp of the topic, they focus their attention on the sounding-out process. In order to offset this tendency, it is very important that we introduce them to the idea that it is more useful to get the sense out of a text than it is to sound out each and every word.

Another reason for encouraging our students to focus on meaning rather than decoding is that only by so doing will they build up any speed in their reading. As we saw in the section on reading theory, fluent readers do not identify every word. They focus instead on the words which carry meaning. Just as Gloria's lawyer knew that expressions

like "shall be seen by these here present" could be safely ignored, so
fluent readers ignore the function words — the support words in a
sentence like **the, was, being,** and **of** — or at a more advanced level,
expressions such as, "Therefore it can be seen that. . . ."

A student who approaches reading as a series of words of equal importance to be sounded out is not prepared to judge which words are
significant, and therefore slows his reading speed down to process every
symbol.

We can see then that there are valid reasons for teaching literacy with
methods which stress understanding of the text. This is not to say that
there is no value in approaches which focus on decoding. Obviously
students need to learn how to decode too; and the most successful
methodology is one which combines both approaches. *What is important is that the student begin with a meaningful text which can later
be used for decoding exercises, rather than beginning with individual
sounds and later building up to complete sentences.*

A good ESL literacy program employs a variety of approaches which
we shall consider in detail. No one approach is valid alone, although
for the sake of clarity we will explore them individually. Later we will
consider ways in which the various approaches can be coordinated.

READING FOR MEANING

There are a number of approaches to teaching reading for meaning.
What they have in common is that the material with which students work
is made up of words in a meaningful context.

The meaningful context may take the form of an entire story which
interests the student, or it may be as small a unit as a sngle word, if
that word is presented in a context where the meaning is obvious. Labels
on washroom doors, or students' names under pictures of them, are
examples of single words in context.

More commonly, sentences are used as the minimum unit. Not only
is more meaningful information given in such a context, but students
become used to handling print in terms of thought units. Their reading
is more fluent when each piece expresses a complete idea, not a string
of unconnected syllables.

At first sight, this concept may seem a little overwhelming. How can
students possibly make sense of an entire sentence if they cannot read
the individual letters or words? In practice what happens is that the
students are told what the writing says and have oral command of it,
and are then asked to work with the words sufficiently to begin to
recognize and remember the words individually. Because they begin
with knowing the meaning of what they are attempting to read, they

can use memory and the sense of the sentence in order to identify the words in it. One of the most effective ways to get students interested in attacking print is to use a text made up of their own oral language. This is commonly known as the Language Experience Approach, or LEA.

The Language Experience Approach

In this approach the students begin with an oral discussion. The topic of the discussion may be a shared experience such as a class trip, or a situation common to many of the students, such as problems on the job. It may focus equally well on areas where the students feel a need for literacy, such as the situation they encounter in banks or in writing notes to the school. Pictures work well as a stimulus for discussion; or the subject could be a retelling of a story read together, or a television program. Any topic of interest to the students can provide the material for this approach. In the course of discussion, students have an opportunity to verbalize their thoughts on the subject and try out their language.

The teacher asks the students to volunteer their thoughts on the subject under discussion. Each student is given the opportunity to offer something. The teacher writes down the students' remarks where everyone can see clearly, for example on a chalkboard, flip chart, or overhead projector. The teacher makes it clear that he or she is writing down exactly what the students say. At the end of each contribution the teacher can read the sentence aloud, running a finger under the words as they are pronounced, and checking with the student that what is written represents what the student said. This reading aloud of the text can also be repeated at the end of each paragraph, if the created story is long enough.

The repeated oral reading of parts of the story serves a number of purposes. It gives the students a chance to revise what they have said if after more thought they feel dissatisfied with their contribution. It refreshes their memory as to the content of what was said, and it strengthens their belief that writing can represent their own words. Above all, the constant repetition enables them to make the first links between visual shapes and known words.

When the story is completed, the teacher reads it aloud again, again with the finger running along below the words. This does not mean that the teacher points to each word and carefully pronounces it. Rather the story is read smoothly, at natural speed, with the finger sliding rapidly along. After the story has been read aloud in its complete form, the students are encouraged to join in another reading of it, reading any part they can remember. Most students remember their own contribution quite well and enjoy reading it aloud. Others prefer to read silently.

Obviously, the less literacy the students have, the less they are likely to identify the visual shapes of words with the oral words. If the LEA stories are kept fairly short in the early days, the students' memory of what they said orally will be stronger, offsetting their lack of familiarity with the letters. At this stage the teacher may read the passage aloud two or three times and then ask students to read aloud any individual words they have identified. Because the students are likely to have a limited vocabulary, some words are certain to be repeated. The teacher might read aloud the sentence in which a word first appears, point to the significant word, and ask students to search the story to find subsequent appearances of the same word. Other students might recognize and volunteer parts of a sentence. If the students are left to work together as a group, they can often piece the story together orally. Under any of these guises, the teacher gets the students familiar with the story and beginning to recognize certain words.

The process just described is the basis of the LEA method. As well as being valuable in themselves, the stories produced provide material for a variety of follow-up activities in both meaning and decoding. Before considering these more fully, let's look at the advantages in learning by the LEA method. First, it is likely to be quite different from any system by which students previously attempted literacy, and is therefore less likely to meet with resistance of the "I've tried this before and I can't do it" variety. Second, it combines the best of both of the major literacy approaches. It begins firmly with language in a meaningful context, but also provides the opportunity for work on decoding which will enable students to tackle new words. Third, it is based on the students' own expressed needs and interests rather than a teacher-imposed topic of

possibly doubtful interest. Finally, it gives ESL literacy students an opportunity to attempt literacy without the added barrier of language problems. The words they attempt to read are their own words; the vocabulary is familiar to them; the syntax reflects their speech patterns; the meaning is firmly based in their own global experience.

It is because of the importance of this last point, the familiar language, that the teacher is urged to write down exactly what the students say, not a corrected form. This does not mean that the teacher should reproduce the student's accent, and transcribe **sheep** for **ship**; the students have no expectation of how the word **ship** should look and won't recognize it any more easily for seeing a phonetic rendering of their pronunciation. They do have an expectation of seeing a pattern of words in a sentence, however, and the story should reflect the syntax that they actually use. Pat Rigg, in her article, "Beginning to Read in English: The LEA Way," (*SPEAQ Journal*, vol. 1, no. 3 (Fall 1977), pp. 60-79) offers these excellent reasons for faithful transcription.

Teachers trying LEA for the first time need to remind themselves that their job is to write what the students say, not, and this is important, not to write what they want the students to say. . . . In order to write what the students say, the teacher has to give them plenty of chances to say something: this means that the teacher must supply time, silence, and attention.

I want to mention another point while I'm talking about writing what the students say rather than what the teacher thinks they should say. If the students dictate something ungrammatical, the teacher must transcribe it as dictated, grammatical mistakes and all. One of my students gave me this sentence from page one of Mayer's *A Boy, A Dog, and A Frog*, "Boy and dog walking."

That's what I wrote, and that's what I said when I read it aloud. "Boy and dog walking." I didn't make any changes, and I didn't make any comments about the grammar.

There are three main reasons for transcribing exactly what is dictated, without any discussion of grammar and without any grammatical "improvements" by the teacher. First, the core of LEA is using the beginning reader's language as the base on which to build reading materials, and that means the *reader's* language, not someone else's. Second, the focus of the lesson should not deteriorate into a presentation of grammatical niceties. Third, transcribing exactly what the students say gives the ESL teacher both a record of progress and data for further lesson planning.

The first reason is the most vital. LEA works when the students' beginning reading materials, developed by the students with the teacher's help, have the student's ideas in the students' language. If it's the teacher's ideas and the teacher's language, it may be marvelous material, but it isn't LEA. LEA works because anyone can read what she has just said. It's more difficult to read what someone else has just said, but it's possible as long as what is said and the way that it's said correspond to one's own ideas and language forms. "Boy and dog walking" are the student's present language forms. If I have to bite my tongue to keep from correcting that sentence, I bite it. Frequently, a student who's more proficient in English will want to correct her classmate's English errors. I do not want and will not allow one student to yell out comments about another's contributions. For a class LEA story (rather than an individual one), when I reread the sentence and ask, "Did I write this correctly? Is this the way you want to say it?" a more advanced student may suggest that "boy and dog" be altered to read "a boy and a dog." When students offer suggestions like this, where one student suggests changing another's sentence, I always ask the original author for permission before changing anything.

The second reason for writing exactly what is dictated is that, if I interfere during the transcription step by changing the language or by making it clear to the students that I expect them to change it somehow, then I am focussing their attention on trivia, on surface forms. My interference suggests, however inadvertently, that reading is really another grammar lesson. I don't want to give my students that impression. I believe reading is going from print to meaning, and I want them to believe that too, and to go for the meaning whenever they try to read anything, rather than lose the meaning because they are concerned with form more than with content. The objection that's frequently made to writing exactly what the students say, incorrect grammar and all, is that the teacher is thus reinforcing poor English by not correcting the mistakes. Maybe, but I don't think so. The teacher is recording and repeating the students' sentences; that may be reinforcing to some students sometimes. And if it is sometimes reinforcing, what is getting reinforced, the contribution of an idea or the format in which the idea was presented? One really cannot tell. Most of the research that's been done on language acquisition has been done with first language learning and may not apply to second language learning, but, in first language learning, the focus is on the meaning, not on the form. If a child says, "Mommy home," and it is her mommy pulling into the driveway, her daddy is likely to say, "Yes, Mommy's home." But if a child says, "Mommy's home," and it's not Mommy, no one compliments the child on her excellent use of contracted *to be*; Daddy says, "No, you're wrong. That's not Mommy." Now, we all learn to speak our first language pretty well, and we do so while attention is directed to content, not to form. Maybe our second language learners can learn ESL while directing their attention to meaning, rather than to form. That is what the teacher is doing when he transcribes what is said without correcting the grammar: he's paying attention to meaning. I hope his doing so will "reinforce" the students' tendency to do the same.

The third reason the teacher-scribe needs to write what's dictated without interfering or changing it is that the students' volunteered sentences, which are recorded in the LEA story, supply excellent information about the students' present proficiency in the language and their progress. (Pp. 62-64)

Not all teachers will agree with this stress on writing down the exact words of the students. Some feel that to write down incorrect forms reinforces the students' mistakes, and confuses other students who thought they knew the correct form. With an adult class it is fairly easy to make clear to the students that the text may well include mistakes, but that the opportunity is always available for the speaker to substitute the correct form. Basically the teacher has to decide what the priorities are for any given exercise. If the main focus is grammatical accuracy, the language should be corrected. If, however, the focus is word recognition, the sentences should be recorded as spoken.

Follow-up Activities to LEA

Almost any of the numerous techniques used in literacy teaching can be developed from the basis of an LEA story, from phonic analysis of words in the story to writing captions for pictures illustrating it. Many of these activities will benefit from having their origins in such a meaningful context. There are, however, some specific techniques which tie in so closely that they are often considered part of the experience approach.

1. When a class has completed the oral reading of a story, the story can be transcribed by the teacher for further work. It should be photocopied, so that each student receives a copy of the story for a file for silent reading later.
2. Students can copy all or part of the story for writing practice.
3. Working with the teacher's transcript of the story, students can underline all the parts which they can read. This not only helps the teacher assess progress, but demonstrates progress to the student.
4. The teacher can transcribe the story leaving blanks to represent certain words (a *cloze* exercise). The blanks can replace certain

types of words, such as nouns, or can be spaced regularly throughout the story. Students then attempt to read the story orally, supplying each missing word or an acceptable substitute. This exercise provides excellent practice in prediction. Students may also tackle the cloze exercise as a writing exercise, although the missing words may need to be provided (in random order) on the blackboard to help with spelling.

5. The teacher may focus on one sentence of the LEA story for further work. The sentence is written on a large strip of card, and individual words in the sentence are written on index cards. The teacher reads the chosen sentence aloud, or asks for volunteers to read it. Students then attempt to match the individual words on the index cards with the master sentence, reading the completed sentence as they do so. In this way students learn to recognize individual words and the way in which they are put together to make a sentence. (It is usually easier if one of the more grammatically sound sentences is chosen for this activity.)

6. The students can be given the cards in random order and work in groups to recreate the sentence with or without reference to the master.

7. The word cards can be rearranged to make new sentences, particularly if one or two extra cards using other words from the story are provided.

Reading for Meaning Using Found Materials

A major value of the language experience approach is that it is based on the students' own language and experiences, and thus provides a very useful way to approach reading. There are many kinds of text which the students will want to be able to read, however, such as street signs, which cannot be developed through the LEA approach. We need to handle this material rather differently, even though our focus will still be on the meaning. Because this type of material comes in so many different formats it is difficult to spell out exact steps for approaching it. We can, however, look at some general guidelines and then consider examples in more detail.

The kind of materials that our students may want to work with include:

memo pads	application forms
school circulars	bank slips and cheques
workplace notices	charge slips
food can labels	bus timetables
food package directions	memos
want ads	telephone directories

street signs	maps
work reports	pharmaceutical instructions
work manuals	popular songs
instruction sheets	

Many of these would be overwhelming tasks for beginning literacy students if presented in their entirety. Our first step is, therefore, to restrict each task in some way. We might choose two or three can labels to begin with, prepare a simplified instruction sheet for a familiar procedure, or focus on one very small section of a job manual. The next stage is to ensure that the students are familiar with the context of the material. They should know where it comes from and what kind of information they are likely to find in it. In the example of the can labels, students will make better progress working with actual cans of food, or at least the actual labels from them, than they would if we carefully typed the content of the labels onto a clean sheet of paper — where all the benefits of context and format are lost.

After restricting the task to a manageable size, the next stage is to familiarize students with the specific content of the material. This usually means that the teacher reads it aloud as many times as is necessary. Alternative procedures include using more advanced students, teacher aides, or a tape recorder to help in this process. Once students are confident that they know more or less what the text says, the focus can shift to individual items in the text. The final stage is to have students manipulate the individual items so that they learn to recognize them in different contexts. **The pattern of approach is therefore to work down from an overall understanding of the text to a specific knowledge of the individual parts.** Let's consider how this could be handled in a classroom, using two examples: one a text which is exclusively for reading, as in following instructions, and one which demands some writing too, such as an application form.

Students who want to be able to follow written instructions need first some familiarity with the kind of format in which the instructions are given. We can restrict the task by beginning with a process which is already familiar to them. We might draw up a simple set of instructions identifying the steps in making a cup of coffee or performing a task which they do at work daily. Or we might make good use of the context provided by the instructions on a package of cake mix. If the literacy work can be related to an end product — such as the class making cookies for the coffee break — it will be highly successful. Not all teachers have baking facilities available, however. An alternative process might be planting seeds following instructions on the package, or following directions on a large-scale map of the neighborhood to find the nearest bank or library.

Whatever subject we choose, we will start with a reading text which is a short set of instructions for a familiar procedure, thus reducing the demands on the students to something they can reasonably expect to succeed at. The next stage is to make them thoroughly familiar with the content. This stage might be handled as a class discussion of what students think the text will say. In the example of the cookie mix, the teacher might ask students to guess what the package contains, and to suggest which ingredients will need to be added, or to guess at the baking time and temperature. This introduces vocabulary items before the students are faced with them in print, and helps their ability to predict. The teacher then gives out the cookie-mix packages to small groups of students to examine. If there are large numbers of students, it may be necessary to give copies of the text rather than actual packages. However, photocopies of the original package should be used if possible, to preserve the format, rather than written-out copies of the directions only.

Students should be given time to thoroughly examine the packages or copies. Most students will be able to use context clues to determine which pieces of writing actually represent the directions. Many will identify the numbers indicating baking time and temperature. Some will begin checking their early guesses as to the procedure, others will wait to hear it read aloud first. When the teacher goes on to read the instructions aloud, he or she may wish to record the reading so that students can replay the tape as many times as they wish while following the text. Students who were not able to check their predictions previously will do so now.

Having become thoroughly familiar with both the general sense of the text and the specific information it contains, the students can now focus on individual parts of the instructions. This can be handled in a number of ways. Students may be asked to volunteer to read certain lines. One set of instructions could be cut up into the individual steps, and shuffled, for the students to resequence. Pairs of students, each one having only a partial text, could piece their information together. Comprehension questions can be asked either by the teacher or by other students, such as "How much water does it need?" Best of all, students can actually make the cookies — the activity guaranteeing their focus on each step in turn.

Follow-up activities might include a cloze version of the instructions which students write out, filling in blanks from a word pool or from the original text. Specific sentences from the text could be taken apart for closer examination, with individual words written on cards in the manner described under Follow-up Activities to LEA. Some words appearing in the text will lend themselves to phonic analysis; for example, **bake, batter** and **butter** to illustrate initial **b**, or **bake** and **make** as the beginning of a word family. Best of all, an LEA story on **How we made cookies** can provide excellent reinforcement of vocabulary and word spellings.

A text such as a form which demands a response in writing is usually handled a little differently. The language is rarely provided in complete sentences and there may be little contextual information, so that the student has to be more accurate in word recognition. What context there is should, of course, be thoroughly exploited.

As an illustration, consider how we might initially handle student interest in completing job application forms. Because such forms vary from employer to employer, and may be rather lengthy, it is probably best if the teacher prepares a simplified version to begin with. The amount of information that can be included will depend on the level of the class, but a good start can be made even with the simplest of personal data. For a class which already knows **name, address,** and **phone no.,** the teacher might develop a form like figure 10.

Although only two new items (date of birth and last employer) are demanded in this form, it covers some important information. Students will become familiar with the box layout of most forms. They will learn the distinction between the use of name and address, without qualifier, to mean their own name and address, and the use of these, under a heading, to refer to someone else. They will also be learning the significance of shaded boxes headed "office use only."

The class might begin with a discussion of how the students cope with application forms, and the kinds of forms they face. The teacher might guide the discussion towards the types of question the students think might be asked on forms, so that they develop expectations of the text. When the students are first given the form, the teacher points out that

APPLICATION FORM		
NAME LAST FIRST OTHER		DO NOT WRITE HERE OFFICE USE ONLY
ADDRESS		DEPT. CODE #
TELEPHONE	DATE OF BIRTH DAY/MONTH/YEAR	PS6 APPROVED
LAST EMPLOYER NAME _____		SECTION SIGNATURE
ADDRESS_____		

Figure 10

this example is only the first part of a form, and that many of the other questions raised by students would be asked in a longer form.

Students are then given some time alone, or in small groups, to look at the form and see if they recognize any of the words. Because forms are so sparse in language terms, there is little contextual help for the students. A useful trick is to show a completed form, so that the handwritten entries give another set of clues as to what is required. This is best done on an overhead projector, where attention can be focussed on individual sections; but it can also be provided on a sheet of paper. The students see the form looking like figure 11, and are immediately aware of which boxes they need to complete and what kind of information is required.

After this, the students return to the blank form and read it through together, identifying the information required. The key words in the form can then be put onto flashcards, to be matched with another set of cards showing answers. Next, the flashcards can be presented alone, to be read aloud. Finally, the students could attempt to complete the form, if necessary copying the information from cards provided by the teacher. Alternatively, students could work in pairs to complete the forms for each other, one asking the questions and transcribing the answers while the other provides the spelling.

APPLICATION FORM

NAME			DO NOT WRITE HERE
SOULATHA BOUNMI			OFFICE USE ONLY
LAST	FIRST	OTHER	
ADDRESS *3400 EGLINTON AV EAST #1206*			DEPT.
SCARBOROUGH ONT. M3T 4P4			CODE #

TELEPHONE	DATE OF BIRTH	
223-6641	*12 JAN 53*	PS6
	DAY/MONTH/YEAR	APPROVED

LAST EMPLOYER	
	SECTION
NAME *CARHART*	SIGNATURE
ADDRESS *12 PROSPECT DRIVE TORONTO.*	

Figure 11

Total Physical Response

Total Physical Response (TPR) is a method which can be successfully adapted for use with literacy classes even in the very early stages. As its name implies, it asks for a physical response to a language item, rather than an oral one — that is, the student carries out the suggested action rather than repeating it or manipulating the language in some way. This method has obvious advantages for students with limited oral proficiency. Students can display their understanding of an instruction without being hampered by their inability to produce an oral response. The teacher can see instantly which students have failed to understand (unlike choral oral responses, where hesitant students are drowned out by more vocal class members). The physical movement helps the student relate the language item to its meaning and reinforces memory. Finally, the opportunity presented for students to move around provides a pleasant change of pace from sitting immobile at a desk.

To use TPR in an ESL literacy class, the steps are as follows:

a. The teacher draws up a list of simple commands which the whole class or group can perform simultaneously; e.g. **Stand up, Smile Go to the board, Write your name, Go back, Sit down.**

b. The teacher acts out the commands while repeating the words orally.

c. The students join in, responding to the oral commands.

d. The students perform the commands several times, in sequence, joining the teacher in saying them orally if they wish.

e. As the students become familiar with the oral form of the commands, they call on each other to act them out.

f. The teacher introduces the commands in written form (preferably on large cards so that the writing can be read easily at the back of the class). As each command card is shown, the teacher reads it and performs the action.

g. The teacher shows each card, pausing a little before reading it aloud, to allow the students time to attempt to recognize it themselves. Students perform the actions first as a group, then individually.

h. The cards are shown alone, still in sequence, without the oral command. The students respond.

i. The cards are then shown out of sequence, and the students respond.

j. The cards are all put on display and the teacher says one of the commands. The students point to the appropriate card.

k. The students write down the commands onto small cards and work in groups, giving instructions to each other.

Valuable as TPR is, it does present one problem in a literacy class. Unless the teacher has unusually good facilities, or is working with a very small group, the commands are limited to such things as moving around the room. This does not always involve the vocabulary items which are normally considered the most immediately useful. Ideally TPR is used to teach instructions which the students need to be able to decipher in print — the steps in using a pay phone, or getting a cup of coffee from a vending machine, for instance. With a small enough group, TPR offers a valuable way of covering such material, but it is unlikely to be feasible for large groups of students.

This problem can be partially overcome if the teacher makes use of easily available props. A set of advertising flyers would enable clothing vocabulary to be covered. Playing cards are useful for numbers. Boxes of crayons can be used to teach colors. To be avoided is too much use of instructions (such as "Shake hands with your neighbors") which students are unlikely ever to meet outside the classroom.

Dialogues

Dialogues have been used in oral ESL teaching for a number of years. A short conversation between two speakers is modelled for the class until, through frequent repetition, the students are familiar with the form and can produce the dialogue themselves. Normally in oral work a particular sentence pattern is featured in the dialogue, and later exercises work on substituting alternative vocabulary items into this pattern (a *substitution drill*).

Dialogues can also be used successfully in a literacy class, although some adaptations are necessary. Dialogues reflect oral speech and may not present material which the students are likely ever to meet in print. The content of the dialogue thus needs to be carefully chosen. Literacy dialogues also need to be short (four to six lines) and include a considerable amount of repetition. For beginning students the focus need not be on presenting a particular pattern, but rather on including a number of useful words supported by the meaningful context of the dialogue. With more advanced students the dialogue offers a very useful way of helping students recognize and manipulate sentence patterns.

The way in which a dialogue is presented varies a little according to the level of the class. If the students have limited oral skills, it will be necessary for the dialogue to be presented orally first until the students have fully understood it. The steps would therefore be as follows:

a. The dialogue is presented orally. If possible a teacher aide plays the second role, to help make clear that there are two speakers. Otherwise the dialogue is taped, or the teacher can use puppets or pictures to indicate the two speakers. The dialogue is repeated several times with as much action as necessary to clarify the meaning.

b. The dialogue is then written up on the board. In each line the teacher leaves blanks to represent certain words, and lets the students call out the appropriate word. It is particularly useful to have blanks representing any unknown words to help focus the students' attention on these words. The teacher then reads the completed dialogue aloud, sliding a finger rapidly under the words as they are spoken.

c. The teacher reads out one role while the class reads the other chorally. Roles are then reversed. After some practice in this fashion, the class is split in half, each half taking one role. As a final step, the students work in pairs reading the dialogue.

d. The teacher erases the words which were originally represented by blanks and asks the students what the words should be. Students can volunteer the words orally, or write them on the board in the appropriate space.

e. The students copy the dialogue into their notebooks.

With a class whose oral skills are more developed, rather than first introducing the dialogue orally the teacher writes it on the board, allowing the students to call out the words as they recognize them. The class then reads the entire dialogue chorally, guided by the teacher's finger sliding under the words. The meaning of the dialogue is then discussed and any implications talked over. As a next step the class can model the dialogue as outlined in (*c*) above; the teacher then erases any words which are felt to be difficult or new, for the students to replace. Finally the students can write the dialogue, using a separate index card for each line. The cards can then be shuffled and re-ordered.

Interviews

Another useful activity, which combines reading for meaning with practice in the other skill areas, is the interview. Interviews consist of setting students the task of finding out information about each other. To

Ask: When is your birthday?   Name _____

Chi Phu _____   1   2   3   4   5   6   7
Hon Vo _____   8   9 10 11 12 13 14
Santos _____   15 16 17 18 19 20 21
Jesus _____   22 23 24 25 26 27 28
My Lan _____   29 30 31
Hourn _____
Shong Gath _____   JANUARY
Yolanda _____   FEBRUARY
Huot _____   MARCH
Ildefonso _____   APRIL
Roberto _____   MAY
Lourn _____   JUNE
Som Lot _____   JULY
Chan Thy _____   AUGUST
                           SEPTEMBER
                           OCTOBER
                           NOVEMBER
                           DECEMBER

Figure 12

Name _____

Ask _____ (teacher completes name of another
student)

"When were you born?"

Answer:_____

Ask _____

Which country do you come from?"

Answer: _____

Ask _____

"What's your address?"

Answer: _____

Figure 13

do this the teacher prepares a worksheet which requires students to ask
each other questions. The questions can be very simple or quite complex, according to the level of the students. Figure 12 gives an example
of an "easy" sheet.

This type of exercise helps the students get to know each other, and
provides practice with such basics as dates within an interesting context. Students also enjoy the opportunity to get up and move around;
and class members who find the task difficult can use this opportunity
to ask others for help in the native language.

At a more advanced level, a sheet like figure 13 can be used.

DECODING APPROACHES

Sight Words

The sight-word approach is a technique which works well with either
a meaning or a decoding approach. The basic technique is to present
a word as a whole and encourage students to recognize it as an entire

word, not a succession of sounds. Much of the approach described in Reading for Meaning leads to the development of sight words, but sight words can be taught in many ways. Any words can be taught as sight words, but the technique is particularly useful for words which are not regular phonetically — words which it would be very difficult to sound out. Some of the most common words in English are not phonetically regular, yet the students will need to recognize them if they are to attempt any reading. Some of these words are **of, to, was, have, one, would,** and **who**. It is also useful to develop certain regular words as sight words so that they can function as a standard for developing word families. As students progress in literacy they will come to recognize more and more words on sight, including words which they initially learned by sounding out. Good readers develop an enormous bank of sight words and rely on them almost exclusively in their reading, sounding out only words which are unknown to them. Encouraging students to recognize sight words sets them on the road to building up such a bank.

You will probably find that your students already have some sight words — **STOP, Coca Cola, Sale,** for instance. They have learned to recognize these by frequent exposure to them in a clearly identified context. Teaching sight words should follow the same pattern — frequent exposure and identifiable context where possible.

Not all potential sight words have a clear meaning attached to them. Some of the words most commonly encountered, such as **have, was, to, are,** and **of,** are extremely difficult to explain or illustrate. In order to provide some context, these words should be presented in a sentence. The sentence could be taken from an oral story given by the students, or from something they want to read, such as a driver's manual. Let's take a sentence such as **You must have a license to drive a car**. If the teacher writes this sentence up on the board and reads it to the students two or three times, they will probably be able to read along, even if they are not able to recognize the words out of context. The teacher may decide that the important words to learn are **have** and **to**, and points these words out, and writes them on small index cards. Students can each be given a card and asked to match the card they have with the appropriate words in the sentence on the board. If the class is too large for this to be feasible, the teacher can provide sheets of paper containing the sentence for the students to work on.

After the students have successfully matched the new sight words, they can be asked to copy each word onto a card. The new words are mixed into a group of cards containing familiar words, and are held up one at a time for the students to read. When the students seem familiar with the new words, they are asked then to close their eyes and try to visualize the words one at a time. They then write the words down and check them against the board to see if they are right. Finally, students can write the new words into the original sentence provided on a sheet with blanks in appropriate places.

New words introduced in this way will need to be reinforced if students are to continue to remember them. The more common words can be included in other reading work; less common ones can be included in the flash card sessions of subsequent lessons.

Sight words are learned by exposure of all types. Reading words in and out of context, writing them, saying them, tracing them, even drawing pictures of them, all help to reinforce the words. Some students need considerably more exposure than others to learn a new word. Often students find the process easier if they can physically manipulate the words by writing them on cards and rearranging them. Suppose the students are trying to learn the days of the week. The teacher puts the task in context by asking students what they have done on specific days. The class might end up with sentences such as

> **John went to work on Monday.**
> **On Tuesday Gina went to the movies.**

If all these words are written on cards, it is easier for the students to form new sentences by rearranging cards than to write out each new attempt. They might rearrange the cards to read

> **Gina went to work on Monday,**
> *or*
> **On Monday, Gina went to work.**

If words such as **and** are in their vocabulary the teacher might provide some extra word cards to create

> **Gina and John went to work on Monday.**
> **John went to work on Monday and Tuesday.**

Using cards in this way gives students a tool to handle the language and gives them the confidence to attempt new sentences. Simultaneously, of course, it reinforces the various sight words and the sentence patterns.

Occasionally a problem will arise over confusion of two sight words which are similar in appearance. Pairs like **was** and **saw** or **then** and **than** often cause confusion. It is usually best to handle this by focussing initially on only one of the pair until that word is thoroughly known, before re-introducing the second word.

Sight words can also be developed without any conscious effort on the part of the students if labels are placed on objects on display in the classroom. Captions under photographs of interest to the class work in a similar fashion. A collage could be built up of photographs of street signs and door labels. As long as the context is clear, the sight word will soon become familiar to the students.

Sight words are clearly a very useful tool for the reader. But because they do not provide help with other unknown words, it is not wise to try to teach exclusively by sight words, as the students will make slow progress. As they become more skilled in using meaning and phonetic clues to unlock new words, they will begin to build up sight words by themselves.

Phonics

No matter how highly developed our skills of prediction may be, we must be able to decode a number of words in any text if we are to confirm our guesses. We can learn to decode words in their entirety or we can approach them letter by letter. Unlike Chinese, where the written symbol gives us no information about the sound which it represents, alphabetic writing systems are based on the principle that the letters represent the various sounds in the word. In some languages, such as Finnish or Turkish, this is almost completely true, and the correspondence between spelling and pronunciation is nearly perfect. In other languages, of which English is a prime example, the correspondence may be rather irregular. Common examples of such irregularity are the various pronunciations assigned to the **ough** spelling, as in **cough, rough** and **bough**. Spellings may represent more than one sound and sounds may be represented by more than one letter or group of letters. With 43 sounds to be expressed by 26 letters, some double duty is inevitable. Despite the many cases of lack of correspondence between sound and symbol in English, there are many many words in English which are perfectly regular in their spelling, and all of the remaining words are at least partially regular. Critics of English spelling have invented the word **ghoti**, pronounced as **fish**, which is made up of the **f** sound from **rough**, the **i** sound from **women**, and the **sh** sound from **nation**. In practice, though, a situation in which a word's spelling has no relation to its sound never arises. Consonants in particular tend to be fairly regular in their sounds. With only a few exceptions, single consonants either make their normal sound or are silent. Thus, despite the irregularities of English spelling, the concept of sound-symbol correspondence is valuable to students and is a necessary tool in developing literacy.

Because of the regularity of spelling of initial consonants and because initial consonants are useful for prediction purposes, many teachers begin their phonics work with them. Most consonants cannot be produced in isolation without distorting the sound, so it is best to teach them in the context of a syllable. There is evidence to indicate that students find it easier to break words into syllables than into individual sounds, so that working with syllables simplifies the learning-to-read process.

Assuming that the students have done sufficient pre-literacy work to be familiar with the letters, the teacher may focus on a chosen consonant such as **b**. In order to ensure that the students hear and recognize the **b** sound, the teacher asks the students to identify whether certain words begin with the sound, as in the outline below.

Initial Consonant Recognition

Teacher holds up or writes Bb.

Teacher says:

This is the letter **B.b.** This is capital B. This is small b.
It makes the sound we hear at the beginning of the word
bank. Listen to these words which begin with **B.**

> bank
> bill
> book
> Bob

Tell me if these words begin with **B.**

> book
> house
> building
> basket
> dentist
> bank

Can you tell me some words which begin with the sound of B?

When students can recognize the letter in initial position, they can be given a similar list of words in written form and asked to circle the ones which begin with **b**.

book
Bob
drive
both
look

It can then be demonstrated, following a similar format, that **b** can appear at the end of a word.

Final Position Consonants

Teacher says:

Listen to the word **rub.** Can you hear the sound of **B** at the end of it? **Rub. Rub.** Here are some other words which end in **B.** Listen for the **B** sound.

fib	tub
sob	cab
dab	crib

Can you hear the letter **B** at the end of those words? Listen to these words and tell me if they end in **B.**

dig	slob
grab	swim
job	cab
sat	

Do you know any words which end in the sound of **B**?

Word Families

Another approach to helping students recognize sound-symbol correspondences is to teach words in families — that is, groups of words which share a number of letters, such as **night, right,** and **light,** or **mean, meat,** and **meal.**

This method is often most successful when it begins with small words with which the students are familiar from other types of reading work. Students may have met and may be able to recognize **and, in,** and **at,** for example. Because they can already read these words, they will find it much easier to tackle other words in the same word families. The familiar word can be presented in an appropriate context to aid student recall, then the teacher can go on to demonstrate how the addition of extra letters forms new words, as in the following outline.

Presentation of Word Families based on Familiar Words

1) Teacher presents familiar word in context. e.g., Menu sign **Special.**

> **Fish and Chips $1.99.**

2) Teacher reads sign. "This says, **Special. Fish and Chips $1.99**"

3) Teacher asks students to read sign, with teacher and then alone.

4) Teacher asks students to find the word **and** and circle it.

5) Teacher says "These letters **a–n–d**, make the word **and.** There are other words which have these letters in them. Can you hear the **and** in these words?

> hand   band   sand   land   grand

We can make all these words by putting extra letters in front of the word **and.**

6) Teacher demonstrates new words by writing appropriate letters in front of **and** on the board.

> If we put **h** in front of **and**, we get **hand.**
> If we put **b** in front of **and** we get **band.** What word do we get if we put an **h** in front?
> And if we put a **b** in front?

What word do you think we'd get if we put an **s** or **sss** sound in front?

7) Teacher works in a similar fashion with other words likely to be familiar orally to students.

8) Teacher provides students with cards with **and** on them and smaller cards with individual letters on. Students put appropriate letters in front of **and** and try out new combinations. Students might work in pairs, making words for each other to read.

9) Students write out the new words they have made.

Student practice with word families can sometimes be made simpler if the teacher prepares index cards with a slider strip for the changing letter, as illustrated below, so that students can slide the strip up and down to make new words.

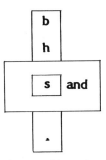

The pattern demonstrated for teaching rhyming word families is also successful for teaching groups of words which end differently. As well as with unrelated words such as **meal, meat,** and **mean,** this technique is useful with common suffixes such as **s, ed,** and **ing,** so that the student manipulates a known word like **work** to make **works, worked,** and **working.** It is useful to focus on suffixes not only because they appear so frequently in reading material, but because the information they provide is often ignored by the literacy student struggling with a second language. In other words we are helping students to get the meaning out of what they are reading, not just recognize the sounds of the letters.

Some of the word families that you might want to cover with students are listed at the back of this book in Appendex B.

THE "IN" FAMILY

7 / Teaching Writing

Reading and writing are, or should be, so closely linked in the literacy class that much of the writing that students do will arise naturally from their reading work. The previous chapter, on teaching reading, demonstrates a number of ways in which students can get writing experience based on their reading activities. Because reading helps students with spelling and word order, they have a better chance of success in writing if the words they are attempting to write have first been reviewed in print. For very basic students this normally implies reading the material and then copying it, using the original for reference. With more advanced students the writing may be a complete reworking of the original text, with sentences rearranged and recombined to form an original piece of work. What both experiences should have in common is an opportunity for the students to review the printed form of the language they intend to use before they attempt to write it.

When students are asked to write, they are asked to demonstrate control of a number of variables simultaneously. In a piece of original writing these variables are **content, format, sentence structure, vocabulary, punctuation, spelling,** and **letter formation.** Beginning literacy students cannot hope for success when attempting to provide all these simultaneously, and yet they need to learn to cope with all of them eventually. The solution is for the teacher to provide control of most of these factors in the early stages and allow the students to focus their attention on controlling one or two aspects of the process.

In the language experience approach, for instance, the teacher takes responsibility for format, letter formation, spelling, and punctuation. The students concentrate on content, sentence structure, and vocabulary. When the students copy out some part of the LEA story, they are focussing on letter formation. A cloze version of the LEA, with certain words blanked out, focusses the students' efforts on letter formation, vocabulary, and spelling. By using exercises of this type, which enable students in the early stages to concentrate on one or two aspects of the writing process, we can provide practice with all the demands without making the task overwhelming.

Activities Focussing on Letter Formation

Most letter-formation practice begins with copying. As we have suggested earlier, copying should be of material which is relevant and meaningful to the students. Oral language provided through LEA is ideal. So is copying relevant personal information, or transferring information from one printed form onto another, the latter exercise providing familiarity with format as well as letter formation. Copying can also be used outside the classroom. Stuents might copy down door signs around the building, or nearby street signs, and then return to class with their writing for a guessing game in which they give other students clues as to where they found the items.

There are a number of advantages to asking students to begin writing with whole words, particularly personal information or their own oral language. In so doing we are strengthening their understanding that writing expresses actual oral language. We are encouraging them to see letters as being grouped into meaningful units, rather than as isolated sounds. However, this focus on a global approach can produce problems if students consistently have problems in accurately reproducing the letter shapes. It may be necessary to backtrack occasionally, to demonstrate letter formation or the placement of letters on a line. We may find for example that having been given a typed copy of a language experience story to copy, students are too faithfully reproducing the typewriter's letter shapes; or that the lack of lines on the typed sheet has not given them sufficient guidance as to where the letters they write should sit in relation to the lines on the page. We would then have to go back to some of the pre-writing activities that provide help with these specific problems.

Forming letters is tiring work for students who have not been used to doing much writing. Often we would like our students to explore written language a little more independently, but find that they get frustrated and tired when attempting new sentences and crossing them out again as problems arise. We can give such students (even those who haven't fully conquered the letter formation process) a chance at attempting more ambitious written material if we relieve them of the task of transcription. The teacher can act as scribe, letting the students use a typewriter, or providing words written on cards which the students can manipulate into new sentences. Providing words written on adhesive labels also works well. Even the old technique of cut-and-paste can provide a welcome relief to hands weary of clutching a pencil; as well as giving the students a break from physical writing, it encourages them to see written language as something which can be manipulated into saying exactly what they want it to say. It even gives them an early introduction to the idea of editing their work.

Working in groups is another way to share the load and help students avoid fatigue over letter formation. Students can work with a series of pictures which tell a story, each student being responsible for writing or copying the caption for only one picture, but sharing the responsibility for checking others' work in such areas as spelling.

Control over letter formation is, however, critical to the writing process, and eventually the students will have to train their hand muscles to cope with fairly lengthy writing passages. Handwriting activities help not only with muscle fitness but also with training the brain to learn certain word and letter patterns. We must therefore provide ample opportunities for physical writing practice, even if this can only be simple copying in the early stages.

As students become more proficient at copying we can increase the demands on them. One thing we might ask them to do is to provide the format. If working with short notes, for example, we might provide a sample letter layout and then ask the students to copy the following text, formatting it to match the sample:

26 Westwood Lane, Toronto. 24 July
1984 Dear Mrs. Davis, Alison was off
school yesterday because she had flu.
Yours, Gianna D'Addona.

Alternatively we might ask our students to provide some of the vocabulary by providing a text with blanks for certain words (i.e., a version of a cloze exercise). The text should be based on language they have produced orally, or material which they have previously read and discussed so that they understand it thoroughly.

The easiest version of this activity provides the missing words in a list in random order and asks the students to select the appropriate word for each blank. Here the focus is clearly on understanding the vocabulary and using it correctly. A more difficult version asks students to choose the appropriate word from a larger pool of words, some of which are not relevant to the passage at all. Finally students can be asked to supply the word from their own memory or understanding of the text. As well as vocabulary, the student at this point has to provide spelling. A still more challenging form of copying gives students the text in a scrambled form. It may consist of sentences with words scrambled or, for more advanced students, sequential passages of up to ten lines, with sentences in random order.

Many beginning literacy students have difficulty recognizing word boundaries, which are difficult to hear in speech; students may write sentences as one long word. A useful copying activity can be made of presenting phrases or sentences run together, such as

Thankyouverymuch,

and asking students to copy them out with the words separated.

If the material which the students are to write is provided orally as a dictation, the demands made on the students increase dramatically. Spelling becomes a major challenge, word boundaries may cause problems, and punctuation may be required. All the teacher provides is content, vocabulary, and sentence structure. Another element introduced is the listening skills of the student. Because of all this and the great handwriting demands it is particularly important that material used for dictation should be thoroughly familiar to the students. Ideally it will be material which they have previously copied, though perhaps rearranged a little. Using spot dictations or cloze exercises is another way of reducing the demands a little: such tasks not only ask the students to write less, but break the task down into a series of small steps. A student can have great difficulty with item 7 but still feel able to attempt item 8. By contrast, a student struggling to transcribe a whole passage is likely to get lost and give up when stumped at word seven.

An effective method of bridging the gap between copying and dictation is to provide the dictation in written form for the students to refer to if necessary. The easiest way to do this is to write each line of text below the space on which the student writes, as in this example.

Please call Mr

Please	call	Mr.	Davies	at	682-1331

He	wants	to	speak	to	you	about

The printed text can easily then be covered with a sheet of paper. Students may attempt the dictation and use the text to check their answers, or read it first, cover it, write, and then check.

Writing practice can also be provided in the form of games and puzzles. Word bingo is one game which works well. Ask the students to draw a grid of nine or sixteen squares, as in Figure 14. Choose a category such as vegetables, body parts, or items of clothing, and have the students put in each square the name of a different item in the category. If necessary provide a selection of words to choose from

hat	coat	socks
shirt	shoes	dress
pants	boots	gloves

Figure 14

on the blackboard. When each student has completed an individualized card, the teacher calls out items and students cross them off on their sheet. The first one with a complete row crossed out in any direction wins.

Crossword puzzles can also be used, although they are not recommended for the early stages of literacy when the students are still struggling with left-right directionality. A little later, however, a simple puzzle with picture clues can provide spelling and writing practice in an entertaining way.

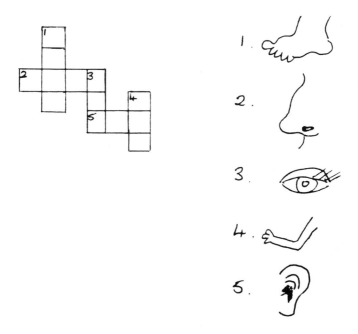

Exercises Focussing on Content and Sentence Structure

As we have suggested earlier, students can focus on the content and sentence structure of writing long before they can form letters, if someone else acts as scribe. The writing need not always take the form of a language experience story. Alternatively, students can dictate original material into a tape recorder, possibly retelling the plot of a movie they have seen, or describing a favorite TV show. If the class includes more advanced students, it may be possible to set up pairs of students with one of the pair dictating and the other transcribing. Good subject matter for such assignments are things like favorite recipes (later to be made into a class cookbook) or short histories of students' lives.

Pictures can also be an excellent stimulus for student work on content and sentence structure. There are a number of books available, of interest to adult students, which provide sequenced pictures illustrating events (see Resources section). Students can work individually with a tape recorder, describing what they see, or as a group, perhaps describing one picture each. More advanced students might attempt to write a caption for each picture, particularly if the teacher provides key words (as in pictures 1 to 4).

1 man morning
   bed gets up

2 bathroom wash
   face towel

3 shave

4 breakfast kitchen coffee

Photographs taken by and of the students are even more useful. Students can be asked to bring in snapshots of their family or their native land, to be captioned and put on the wall as a collage. Photographs of a class trip provide an excellent opportunity for practice in sequencing events. After thorough oral discussion of the event, the photographs can be arranged as an illustrated story, each person being responsible for writing — or dictating and copying — the text for one photograph.

At a more advanced level, students need practice in selecting essential content and arranging it in acceptable sentences. A good example of such tasks is taking phone messages. If the student hears "Hi, this is Susie. Can you ask John to call me back when he gets in?" the task of writing the message is much harder than that involved in simple dictation, even though the information is the same. Students must decide which parts of the message need to be recorded, and rearrange the material in acceptable sentence structure and format. As a way of restricting the writing demands of this task, it could usefully be combined with learning how to use office message pads.

Other forms of note-taking that are useful for students to learn involve asking for information and noting down the main points given. We might ask our students to phone for specific transit information, and report back with the answers; or to call a movie theatre and jot down titles of movies and the times of the performances. Tasks of this

sort obviously demand practice with taped calls before the students are asked to cope with live operators at the other end.

Work on sentence structure can be provided by giving students scrambled sentences to sort out and copy. Ideally the words are provided on cards which the students can rearrange to get the feel of the sentence before they write it out. Alternatively, students can be provided with a pattern sentence into which they slot various substitution words. They might begin with a sentence from their oral work, or a text they have previously read, so that the meaning of the original sentence is clear to them. For example, the students might produce the sentence

She was wearing a big hat.

Initially the teacher would check their familiarity with this pattern by giving them the sentence on cards for re-ordering.

The students can then be given substitution cards to place in the sentence. At an elementary level, these cards might all be designed to slot into one place, a series of adjectives to replace the word **big**, for instance. At a more advanced level, alternatives can be provided for all the words in the sentence, to create new sentences on the same pattern, such as **John is carrying the red box**. If we were to ask students to *write* out all the various different sentences which can be produced with these substitutions, they would find the task very tiresome. Manipulating cards, and perhaps reading the created sentences aloud, reinforce the structure without demanding too much in terms of letter formation.

Activities Focussing on Spelling

Any activity involving print, either reading or writing, helps students with the process of spelling. We learn to spell by frequent exposure to words, by which our brains learn to recognize and produce the correct group of letters for a given word. All our literacy activities therefore benefit the spelling process. But there are activities which have spelling as their primary focus, and most students will need some of them.

One of the first hurdles to overcome is the students' fear of making a mistake. Many literacy students who happily copy from a text stop dead when asked to attempt a word relying on their own resources. We need to encourage students to take risks and at least attempt new words, employing various strategies that we can give them. These strategies include *a*. trying to decide from its sound which letter a word begins with, and at least getting that down;

b. putting down any other letters which they know they can hear the sound of;

c. breaking the word into syllables for possible clues;

d. thinking of rhyming words that they know how to spell (e.g., attack **now** by analogy with **how**), or which begin in the same way (e.g., attempt **real** by comparison with **read**);

e. reading back what they have so far, to see what it sounds like;

f. asking somebody for help;

g. using a dictionary.

If we are to encourage students to be risk takers, it is important that they don't feel that an incorrect spelling is a failure. It helps if we make it clear to students that sometimes English spelling is simply irregular, and that the one spelling accepted by convention as being correct is merely one of a number of alternatives, each of which would be phonetically valid.

A number of techniques are available to help students learn the spelling of particular words. Because people learn in different ways, not all of these techniques will work equally well with any given student. Some students learn best by visual stimuli; they need to look at a word in print, and attempt to put a photograph of it in their memory. For others, sounding the word out is more useful, much as a native speaker might mutter **a-lu-mi-ni-um** to check on letter order. Writing a word out numerous times is a technique which works for many learners. Others prefer a more analytical approach, thinking of the meaning of the base word and adding on suffixes and prefixes.

If a student appears to rely heavily on one particular strategy it is useful to present new words in a format which complements this. In working with a large group of students, however, the best tactic is to provide opportunities for using all the senses to attack new words. We might therefore draw their attention to the word; suggest that they sound it out carefully, noticing which letters are used; close their eyes and try to visualize the word; then look again for confirmation. Finally they can attempt to write the word without looking at the original, check back, and if necessary write it again.

When students are copying new words in the early stages, they tend to look at the text, write down the first letter, look at the text again, attempt the second letter and so on. This does not give as much help in learning spelling as trying to copy an entire word, or at least an entire syllable, at one time. The brain needs to see letters as meaningfully grouped, if the spelling is to be remembered; it is wise therefore to encourage students to attempt copying an entire word at a time.

Some of the ways in which we can make attempting spelling easier involve giving the student part of the required information. We might give words in which only certain letters are missing (e.g., **The __us is stop__ing**). We might provide all the letters of the word, but ask the student to order them correctly. Word jigsaws work well in the early stages, using a cut-up index card for each word.

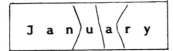   

As students advance, the help provided by physical format can be reduced, and the card cut in straight strips.

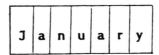

Another way of giving help is to indicate the number of letters in the word, as in this exercise on opposites.

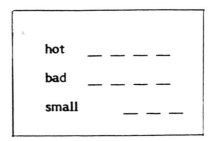

Crossword puzzles provide the same kind of information, and also help with certain letters. Sometimes it is a good idea to provide a crossword with a few of the letters already completed, to help students get started.

Word search games also help students focus on spelling, although in literacy classes it is best to have all the words written horizontally, as in this example on parts of the body:

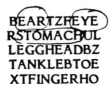

Asking students to keep a personal word dictionary is also useful for spelling, as well as for making them familiar with alphabetical order. Many teachers find file cards ideal for this purpose, as new words can be easily placed in the right order. Others prefer a small address book with pages already labelled for each letter. Because students often like to try to study a few new words in their own time — while riding the bus, for example — it is useful if the dictionary is small enough to be carried around easily.

Word families are not always as useful a tool for second-language learners as they are for native speakers, but the approach can be used with some success, so that a student learns a whole group of new words simultaneously. As with reading, it is most useful to begin with a known word like **in**, which is then expanded to include **bin, chin, thin,** and any other related words in the students' oral vocabulary.

To sum up, students need opportunities and strategies to attack words in many different ways. Above all, they have to be prepared to take a chance, which they will only do in a supportive environment. The more they read and the more they write or attempt to write, the easier they will find the process of reading and writing.

8 / Teaching Multi-level Classes

Even those teachers fortunate enough to begin a course with a class of students with comparable levels of skills are likely to find that after a few weeks some students have made more rapid progress than others, since such factors as first-language literacy and oral competence affect the learning patterns. Most teachers do not even begin with a class designated as a literacy class. Rather, they have a general ESL class with a sprinkling of "literacy" students struggling to follow.

The reality, then, is planning for a wide range of abilities. There is no doubt that sometimes the best solution is to break the class up into smaller groups working at different levels, or pairs of students progressing at their own pace. Even individual assignments may be necessary sometimes.

The solution does not have to be group work, howver. A number of the teaching methods we have looked at so far are quite suitable for use with multi-level groups, if all members of the class fall into the basic ESL category.

Basic Teaching Methods

The Language Experience Approach (see page 45) is one useful method. Students contribute according to their oral competence, reading back those parts of the story within their capabilities. The same LEA story can help one student learn sentence patterns while another student is still working hard at recognizing individual words. Because the beginning student is never being asked to read the entire passage, there is no sense of failure in finding so many words undecipherable; rather there is pride in making out any part of it.

Another basic technique which works well in multi-level classes is Total Physical Response (see page 55). More advanced students will respond quickly to the commands, thus providing further demonstrations of meaning for the beginning students. Because TPR calls for no oral response, students who are weak orally but have a fair passive knowledge will enjoy demonstrating their prowess.

Interview questionnaires (see page 58) are another method suitable for mixed-level groups, as students can proceed at their own pace. The more advanced student will interview every class member, possibly even recording answers in complete sentences, while the beginning student will be equally challenged by the task of identifying and getting a response from four or five individuals. If the spread of abilities is very wide, a second section can be provided on the sheet, to be attempted only if the main exercise is completed. As an example, consider a class working with the question "What did you have for breakfast?" The further task could consist of manipulating the data in some way, for example: "Which students ate eggs?", "Which was the most popular drink?" and so on. Alternatively, it could send the students back to the interviewing process to get more information: "Who cooked the breakfast?", "What did you eat for lunch?" Or it could extend the original question to include people outside the classroom — secretaries, other teachers, janitors, and so on.

Shared Tasks

Even when the range of skills in the group is very wide, there are a number of tasks which can be attempted by the class as a whole that provide opportunity for all students to contribute at their own level. Students might be asked to search the newspaper to find some specific item of information, the literacy students spending most of their time on the first part of the task: identifying the *correct section*. The class might be given bus and train schedules and asked to plan a trip, with basic-level students having responsibility for identifying the *price* from a fairly simple flyer. Making a class "newspaper" (to be pinned on a bulletin board) can be a regular activity providing valuable language practice for a class with a wide spread of abilities. While the more advanced students are writing articles, the others can be writing captions for photographs, comic strips, agony columns, horoscopes, and headlines. Quite apart from the language displayed in the end product, such a process of organizing and producing a project is very useful linguistically. Making photostories or captioned collages are other projects in which students can enjoy working together but can choose tasks to suit their own skills.

Teams

Splitting the class into teams that compete to complete a task correctly is a very easy way to provide motivation and to make sure that basic students join in general classroom activities. Simple tasks such as spelling bees, with the teacher assigning spelling words according to the student's abilities, give a chance for even the most basic student to contribute to the team's success.

Other team games suitable for mixed levels include those in which cognitive skills are as important as language skills — solving puzzles, for example, or variations on Kim's Game, in which the teacher shows a large, detailed picture for about five seconds, and each team then tries to write down everything they can remember in the picture, using words, phrases, or sentences (to get extra points).

Group Work

Valuable as whole-class activities can be, students usually need also to attempt work designed particularly for their level. This normally involves breaking a class into groups.

The most common groupings are *ability groupings*, in which all students in the group have approximately the same level of ability and can attempt a task jointly or individually with the same general explanation and instructions. By this method the teacher can set the same task at the different levels of difficulty, or can set tasks giving practice in different skills according to the needs of different groups.

As an example, let's consider a class working on a theme of health care. Following oral work on getting a prescription from the pharmacy, the teacher might want the whole class to work towards being able to read the instructions on the label. The depth to which this can be achieved will obviously vary according to the student's level, so that the teacher will group by reading ability. While the most advanced group works with manufacturers' labels, and the intermediate group with prescription instructions, the beginning literacy students might be doing an exercise matching poison symbols with words, or instructions about timing and dosage with illustrations of clock faces.

Alternatively, the teacher might group the students according to their need to practise a particular skill, setting up one group to role-play a telephone call to the pharmacy, a second to do listening work with a tape of a doctor giving instructions on the use of medication, while a third group works with a series of photographs related to the theme, sequencing them and writing captions.

Breaking the class into groups in this way can give all the students a chance to do work that is relevant and challenging, but still offers them a chance to experience success. For this reason, grouping is an indispensable technique for the teacher with a multi-level class, even though it often demands a great deal of preparation. Most teachers find it well worth the time spent.

In the examples we have considered so far, the small group functions much like a traditional class in that the teacher sets a task, demonstrates or explains it, and then leaves the students to attempt the work more or less individually while the teacher gives instruction to another group. The grouping is done only to produce a homogeneous group, the actual size being irrelevant. There are, however, many activities which are very much more satisfactory with a small group — discussion, role play, problem solving, and so on. Often for this type of interactive activity, *cross-ability grouping*, where advanced and basic students are mixed together, is more valuable. The advantages in oral work are easy to see, but this type of grouping can also be useful for tasks focussing on reading and writing practice.

Any of the tasks suggested for the whole class, such as planning a field trip or writing a class newsletter, can be usefully given to a small group. Such a group might attempt to put out a recipe sheet, for instance. The basic students could dictate favorite recipes orally for the more advanced students to transcribe. Other students could be involved in layout, making fair copies of rough drafts, proof reading, and so on. Ideally the teacher would allow the group to work out the division of labor by themselves.

Another area where cross-ability groups are particularly useful is in board games. Most commercial games involve a fair amount of reading practice, and many can be adapted to feature language the teacher wants to see covered. With a mixed-ability group, reading problems do not paralyse the entire game, and the element of chance evens out linguistic differences.

Pair Work

Pairing students is useful if the teacher wishes all the students to attempt a particular task but knows they will need varying amounts of time. Normally all pairs of students are given the same task to do, as the logistics of organizing pairs to do different tasks wastes too much lesson time.

Pair work gives students the advantage of working at their own pace; of having someone to give them confidence, to interact with and learn from; and of having the obligation to perform. The latter is an important experience for students who do not feel capable of performing before the whole class. There are a host of activities which two students of similar level can do, from putting their heads together over a discrimination exercise to leafing through a catalogue. Many of the tasks normally allocated as individual work are approached more enthusiastically if set as a pair task.

Many activities rely on the pair arrangement. Pair activities useful for literacy students include interviewing one another and recording the information; sorting and matching sets of symbols and shapes; and holding up flash cards for one another to identify. A particularly useful task is one asking the paired students to pool some information which is given in part to each of them, as in the example. (Each student keeps the given sheet hidden.)

Student A Sheet			Student B Sheet		
	MENU			MENU	
1	Hamburger	1.50	1	Hamburger	
2	Hot Dog		2		1.00
3		.75	3	French fries	.75
4	Coffee	.60	4	Coffee	

By asking questions such as "How much is the hot dog?", "What is number 3?" both students try to complete the menu.

Pairing advanced students with basic students is usually more valuable for speech activities than for literacy ones. It is of course possible to give such an unmatched pair the task of planning something, or producing a letter, but in practice the advanced student either does the task entirely, or else takes the role of tutor so seriously that the basic student makes progress at the other's expense. It is not that involving more-advanced students in some tutoring is never to be recommended, but the tutoring should preferably not encroach on the student's own study time.

Mostly, the unmatched pair arrangement is useful for cooperative games in which both students are trying to achieve the same goal, but the demand is much greater on one of the pair. The basic student may, for instance, have to arrange some cut-out letters to duplicate the arrangement shown on a master sheet held by the advanced student, who must provide detailed verbal instructions. This type of activity provides excellent oral and aural practice for both students, but is not easily adapted to reading and writing. The teacher may prefer to make use of equal-ability groups, or else plan individual activities for the basic-level students.

9 / Combining the Various Approaches in the Classroom: Some Sample Lesson Sequences

As we have said earlier, there is no one perfect method for teaching ESL literacy students. All the various methods have value, and all present strategies which are useful to the student. What we need to do, therefore, is to consider ways in which these strategies can be combined in the classroom.

Pulling the different methods together produces new problems for the teacher. How do we combine them? How long should be spent on one activity? What makes one approach better than another for a particular topic?

To illustrate ways in which the various methods can be put to use in the classroom, we shall look at some sample lessons in detail.

EXAMPLE ONE: A WORKPLACE ESL CLASS

Type of class. A group of 14 women are in an "ESL in the workplace" class. The women all work in a garment factory and attend English classes during their lunch hour. They are mostly of Italian and Portuguese background, with an average education level of grade 4–5. Ages range from 22 to 54.

Literacy level. The women are familiar with the alphabet but have little reading ability in either the native language or English. They never use English in writing, and avoid reading wherever possible.

Language level. Most of the women can express themselves orally although with many mistakes. Very few have had any formal English teaching prior to joining this workplace class but picked up their English on the job.

This class began by focussing initially on oral language. It soon became apparent to Jane, the teacher, that the students wanted to learn to read and write. She has, therefore, been working with the students in this area, and has reached the point where they recognize a number of sight words and will guess at new words, usually on the basis of the initial letter plus context.

Jane's basic plan for the present lesson is to develop an LEA story to be used for both reading and writing practice. She wants to do some work on word families, and introduce the students to the use of final consonants as a decoding clue.

The lesson begins with informal greetings and chat, as the students arrive individually. One woman complains that her fingers are sore, which she says is a result of sewing heavy denim cloth rather than the cord which she usually works with. The other women agree, and point out other problems they encounter with the heavier cloth. Jane realizes that this is an excellent topic for a language experience story, and encourages the discussion. The women explain that they find the denim slower to work with, and consequently do not make as much money on piecework even though the rates have been adjusted. When the subject has been thoroughly talked over, Jane asks the women to say things she can write down on a flip chart.

Some problems become apparent immediately. Many of the volunteered sentences are phrased in the first person. "I go more slow on denim." "My fingers, they get very sore." I and **my** were not volunteered by the same person. Will this fact cause confusion when the material is read back? Jane handles the problem by writing: Gianna says: "My fingers, they get very sore." Many fragments are volunteered. "Too hard". "Denim slow". Jane doesn't change the words, but she does try to guide the fragments into a meaningful context by saying, "O.K., let's make this first part about what the denim feels like, and the second part about the way it slows you down. Anna, what did you say about the way the denim feels?"

Finally the class comes up with this reading text:

Today we sew denim not cord. Gianna says:
"I no like denim. My fingers, they get sore."
Denim is very stiff. Too hard. The denim, it
go very slow through the machine. Anna says:
"Today I break two needle."

It hard to make rate on denim. Janina she
make hundred thirty percent on cord, but
denim she no make hundred percent.

In writing the story out, Jane has corrected the obvious pronunciation errors in the speech; for example, "unnerd tirty percent" is written as "hundred thirty." She has not corrected the grammar, although she has made a mental note of the regular errors, such as the use of a noun and a pronoun for sentence subjects (e.g., **The denim, it** . . . and **My fingers, they . . .**) and the problem with tenses and subject–verb agreement. She may work on these in later lessons, but for now her focus is on reading and writing.

As Jane wrote each sentence on the flip chart, she read it back to the class. "Anna says: Today I break two needle. Is that right, Anna? Is that what you wanted to say?" One of the other students calls out here, "Two needles. It should be two needles." Jane asks Anna, "Do you want me to change it?" Anna looks puzzled and repeats, "Today I break two needle." Jane leaves it as it is.

When the story is complete, Jane reads it back to the class twice. Everyone remembers "Today I break two needle" and joins in on that part. Some students remember most of the text. Jane asks the class what they would like the story to be called, and they agree to call it simply **Denim**. She asks if anyone can find the word denim in the story; this they all can do. One of the students volunteers to copy the word onto the top of the sheet as a title. Another student decides that she wants to change her part a little and tells Jane her new sentence.

Jane then asks for volunteers to read aloud parts of the story. The more confident students volunteer first, while the others wait to hear the material one more time to check that they have it right before they attempt it. A couple of students do not volunteer anything. Jane asks them if they can find particular words, choosing words like **fingers**, in which the initial consonant is a strong clue.

Jane then copies the sentence "My fingers, they get very sore" onto another sheet of a flip chart, which she lays on the table. She also copies each word of the sentence onto a separate index card. She gives one card each to six of the students and asks them to lay the cards over the appropriate word on the flip-chart page. All the students are given an opportunity to match the words in this way, reading the sentence aloud as they do so. Then she takes the master sentence away and asks the students to arrange the cards so as to make the sentence.

When the students can do this easily, she holds up individual word cards and asks "What word is this?" Then she arranges the sentence with one card face down, and asks the students what that word should be.

My	fingers	they	get	very	

She does this a number of times, focussing their attention on different words in the sentence. When she comes to the word **get** she asks the students how they think it should be spelled before she turns it up. After the students have seen the card and checked their spelling, she turns it face down again and asks them to try and write the word. Deciding to do some work with word families, based on **get**, Jane shows the students how the ending of **get, -et**, can be used with other consonants to make new words. The class covers **let, met, set,** and **wet,** all of which are in their oral vocabulary. Jane does not attempt to teach **bet, net,** and **pet**, because they would involve too much explanation, but points out that the words covered are only some of the ones following this pattern. She writes **et** on the blackboard, and the letters **w, s, m,** and **l,** and asks students to make up combinations for others to read. The students write these words down.

Jane then returns to the sentence made up with cards, and reads it aloud again. Because she is going to use this sentence as the basis for making a number of other sentences, she decides that it is necessary to correct the grammar. Without going into detailed grammatical explanations, she says simply, "Let's make the sentence shorter. We don't need **they.** Let's take it out. What does the sentence say now?" After the students have read the new sentence, she asks, "Do you ever get sore anywhere else?" Various aches and pains are described and she writes out cards for **legs, feet, hands,** and **eyes.** The students then arrange one of these new cards into the sentence to produce "My legs get very sore"; and so on. Some of the students have problems with the new words, so Jane draws scribble sketches of the appropriate body part on the back of the card. All the students write the sentence into their notebooks, some copying carefully, others working mostly from memory. As a final wrap-up for this session, the class goes back to the story and reads it aloud one more time.

Before the next class, Jane types out the LEA story and makes copies for the class. She also makes another version which has blanks in it, like this:

Today we sew _____ not cord. Gianna says: I no _____ denim.
My fingers, they get very ___. Denim __ very stiff. Too hard.

The denim it go very ___ through the _____. Anna says: Today
I break two _____.

It hard to make _____ on denim. Janina she ___ hundred thirty
percent on ___, but denim she no ___ hundred percent.

Beginning the next lesson with the first sheet, the complete text, Jane asks the students to spend five minutes with the story and underline any words they can read. Some students underline nearly all the story. Others recognize the names, a few words like **denim,** and the sentence

they worked on in the last session. At the end of the class Jane will
ask them to go through the sheet again, so that they can see their progress. The students will keep these copies of the stories in a file, and
the underlining or lack of it will also demonstrate their long-term progress when they review the stories in a few months.

After the class has had a chance to refresh their memories with the
full text, Jane asks the students to put it away and look at the version
with the blanks. Working through this orally, she asks students to suggest words that might fill the gaps. Not all the suggestions are for words
that were in the original, but so long as they make sense Jane accepts
them; for instance, one student suggests that it's hard to make money
on denim, rather than the rate or quota which was in the original. As
students suggest words which could fill the slots, Jane writes them on
the blackboard. She then asks students to complete the story in writing.
Most of the students simply fill in the blanks on the copies, using the
pool of words on the blackboard for spelling information. Two of the
more advanced students copy the entire story into their books.

Using the modified sentence, "It's hard to make money on denim,"
Jane works with substitutions for various words. The students come
up with "It's easy to make money on cord", "It's hard to make time
on denim", and so on. All these sentences are written on the board,
showing the pattern. Students come up to the board and wipe out certain words, writing in the substitutions suggested by other students —
with Jane's help on spelling, if necessary. Some confusion arises over
e, a, and **i,** as the students mix up the names of these letters. Jane goes
over them one more time. She then asks the students to look closely
at the word **make,** close their eyes, and see if they can imagine the
letters in the word. The students try to write the word, then look back
at the board to check. Jane demonstrates how word families can be made
by changing the end of a word, too, and asks them to listen for the **may**
sound in **make, male, made** and **mate.** She writes up **ma__e** on the
board, and the letters **k, d, t,** and **l.** Working orally, she asks the students
what words will be made if she adds each of the different letters. Some
queries arise over the meaning of some of the words, and Jane sidetracks
a little to put some of the words in context, with examples such as:
"I usually make 130 percent. Last week I made only 100 percent."
"My mate is a male" produces laughter when explained. More usefully, she demonstrates the way the word **male** is used on forms, and draws
a quick sketch on the blackboard, thus:

Name	Jane	
Male	_____	Female ✓

Coming back to the main topic of the lesson, Jane decides to do some work on numbers, using the sentence "I make 130% on cord" as a base. The women are familiar with the percentage system as this determines their wages and is part of the incentive scheme at the factory. All the women volunteer their current percent rates, and they build up a group of sentences on the board, working on quick recognition of the numbers. The students write their own sentences in their books.

Finally Jane asks them to return to the original copy of the story and underline any extra material that they can now read. By this time most of the students are underlining at least half of the story. Jane is aware that not all these words could be read out of context, but is pleased with their confidence, and knows that many of the same words will crop up in subsequent stories for reinforcement.

EXAMPLE TWO: AN EVENING COMMUNITY CLASS

Type of class. There are 19 students in this evening class, 12 men and 7 women. Countries that are represented include Iraq, Yugoslavia, Italy, Greece, Laos, and Vietnam. Most of the people are in their thirties or forties.

Literacy level. Most of the students are at the semi-literate stage. They know the alphabet and understand that the symbols represent specific sounds. However, they use written English only in very limited circumstances, such as certain tasks at work.

Language level. Oral language levels are very mixed in this class. Some students are quite fluent, others have a hard time making themselves understood.

This evening class is identified as a general ESL class. David, the teacher, has found that the variety of levels makes it difficult to do many activities which involve the class as a whole, and he relies on group work a great deal to keep all the students working at a suitable level. For the present sequence of lessons, David wants to cover basic banking procedures.

He begins the first lesson with a humorous account of wasting his lunch hour waiting in a bank line-up. Gradually the students join in and talk about their own problems in using banks. One Italian student comments that his strategy is simply to explain verbally to the teller what he wants and let her fill in all the forms. He adds that he'd like to be able to pay for things by cheque, but always uses a charge card because he doesn't know how to write cheques. Other class members say that they let members of their family do the banking for them, or ask to be paid in cash.

David tells the class that that evening they are going to learn how to write cheques. After making sure that everyone knows exactly what cheques are used for, he holds up a cheque and asks the class what information they think a cheque will have to contain. (In previous lessons with the class David has made the point that most successful pieces of written communication answer the questions **Who, What, When, Where,** and sometimes **Why**.) When the class has trouble deciding what should appear on the cheque, he reminds them of those key words, and the classsoon comes up with:

<u>Who</u> gets the money?
<u>What</u> (how much) do they get?
<u>When</u> is the money paid?
<u>Where</u> will they get the money from?

Why, the class decides, is not relevant to this particular piece of writing. One student volunteers that there is a second **Who** in this case — who pays the money; so that the class list of crucial information goes up on the blackboard as **who the cheque is paid to, date, place, how much,** and **signature**. With this framework to guide their expectations, David shows an overhead transparency of a blank cheque.

```
 _____
|                                                    |
|      MAPLE BANK                                     |
|      Centre St. Branch                             |
|      Blocktown,Ont.        _____ 19 ____     |
|                                                    |
| Pay to the                                         |
| order of  _____ $_____ |
|                                                    |
| _____ DOLLARS  |
|                                                    |
| ACCOUNT NO._____      _____ |
|                                                    |
|_____|
```

David begins by asking the class if they can identify where any of the items of information should go. The dollar sign tips most of the students off, as the slot for "how much." "How about the date?" asks David. "What year is it?" and the figure 19____ becomes significant. David lets the students do most of the work, fitting their expectations of the text to the actual sample in front of them. When they have discovered that they can in fact make a fair amount of sense of it, he steps in to clarify certain points, such as the location (place) already provided in print, and the necessity for writing the amount in both words and figures. He then writes sample entries on the transparency, choosing the simple figure of ten dollars for this initial example. He gives out sample cheques for the students to fill in themselves, asking them to copy this format except for the signature. For the more advanced students, he then gives out a sheet of instructions for writing further cheques:

Write out cheques for these things:
You buy a twenty-dollar sweater at Eaton's on January 31st.
You pay a gas bill of eighty dollars to Consumers' Gas on Feb. 2nd.
You give your friend (any name) a cheque for twenty dollars today.

While the more advanced students are working on this exercise and checking each other, David takes the other students in a group, and they work together on the assignment, using the transparency for reference.

One of the problems David expects soon arises. Very few of the students know how to spell out the numbers. To provide practice in writing numbers in an interesting fashion, David has prepared a bingo game, with laminated cards which can be written on in washable marker and wiped clean after use. He brings the class together to play this game in pairs, with the more advanced students paired with beginning students. When David calls out a number the students have to write the number, in words, in the appropriate square. Correct spellings are provided at the side of the card. Winners are the first pair of students to complete a row correctly. After playing this game with the whole class for ten minutes, David pulls out the stronger students and lets the others continue the game on their own.

For the more advanced students he sets up an activity using sale catalogues. Students work in pairs, selecting items from the catalogue, writing cheques for their purchases, and handing the cheques to their partners for scrutiny. To improve the students' skimming and scanning skills, David incorporates into this activity a role play in which one partner is a customer, wanting (for instance) a red dress, size 10. The other partner must search the catalogue for an appropriate item and announce the price. By the time this activity is running smoothly, the lower-level students are becoming restless at Bingo, and David moves them on to a simplified version of what the other students are doing. He gives them cards, each of which shows an item, its price, and the amount spelled out in words. They complete cheques on the basis of the information on these cards.

For the final ten minutes of the lesson, David works again with the class as a whole, practising orally the kind of language which is involved in writing a cheque. Together they build up a brief dialogue, incorporating such phrases as "Cash or charge?" "I'd like to pay by cheque, please." "I'll need two pieces of I.D." The class ends with a discussion of what constitutes acceptable identification.

In the next class David wants to cover withdrawal and deposit slips. He deals with withdrawal slips first, explaining them as being like cheques paying cash to yourself. He follows a procedure similar to the one used in introducing cheques, calling on students to predict what information is likely to be required. He points out that whereas cheques may be personalized and pre-printed with the person's account number, withdrawal slips are the same for everyone who walks into the bank, and therefore need to have a specific account identified. He encourages the students to always think about what can be expected in a piece of writing, and to look for those elements rather than dive straight into a welter of new words. He points out the importance of finding key words — in this case, the boldface phrase **WITHDRAWAL — all accounts** printed at the bottom of the form. He gives groups of students a selection of forms from various banks, asking them to pull out all the withdrawal slips. Then he asks students to compare the forms from different banks to see if they follow the same format. Some minor changes in layout are noticed, but the students have little difficulty in recognizing which slots are intended for date, signature, amount, and so on. David asks everyone to make out a slip to withdraw fifty dollars. Once more the spelling of the numbers causes problems, so David pulls out the bingo game again for a short (ten-minute) session.

David then breaks the class up, giving some deposit slips to the more advanced students with instructions to see what they can make of them, using the strategy of **prediction** and **confirmation**. With the other students he checks the withdrawal slips they have completed, and asks them to transfer the same information onto a slip for a different bank. This provides handwriting practice as well as experience with different formats. David gives them a task of doing two more slips for different amounts, and sets them up with partners to compare the finished products. Then he goes back to the more advanced students to see how much sense they have made of the deposit slips. They talk as a group about how the slips can be used for simple deposits or for the more complex transaction of depositing cheques and taking part of the funds in cash. Letting one of the students work as scribe, David guides them through the completion of a deposit slip. He then gives them a batch of the cheques they completed in the last class, and asks them to fill out a deposit slip for each amount, while he checks on the other students.

Spelling the numbers out is still a problem for many of the students, and David decides that this needs more work. Because context is not much help in working out exactly which number is referred to, David approaches the words on a straight decoding basis. He decides to get

the students reading the various words easily first, then writing them.
He puts the spelled-out form of the numbers one to ten on index cards
and gives them to the beginning group to put in order. For the more
advanced group, he puts a variety of random numbers between one and
a thousand on cards, and asks them to sort them into numerical order.
Once this is done he tells students in each group to choose a card and
hold it up for the others to identify. When students hesitate he suggests
that they look at the initial letter — it begins f; what can it be? He then
writes the numbers on the board, as in the example.

			---teen		---ty
1	one	11	eleven		
2	two	12	twelve	20	twenty
3	three	13	thirteen	30	thirty
4	four	14	fourteen	40	forty
5	five	15	fifteen	50	fifty
6	six	16	sixteen	60	sixty
7	seven	17	seventeen	70	seventy
8	eight	18	eighteen	80	eighty
9	nine	19	nineteen	90	ninety
10	ten	20	twenty	100	hundred

David shows the students how easy the numbers six to nine are, and
points out that except for the **t** in **eight**, they don't change when **-teen**
or **-ty** are added. Students start to copy the chart down while he is talking, and he gives them time to finish. Then he sets up an exercise in
which students complete the written form of numbers. Early examples
are quite simple and can be done by all the class (e.g., 6 si__).
Gradually they get harder, to keep the more advanced students challenged
(e.g., 200 t____ h_____). The final examples give almost
no help (e.g., 682 ____ _____ and _____ _____).
The class complete as many of these as they can in about 15 minutes.
Some students ask if they can take the sheet home and finish it, using
the chart as a guide.

David then brings the class back to work focussed more on meaning,
with a short written acount of the bank story he had told them in the
last class. He has built into the story many of the words they have met
in their work on cheques and bank slips, such as **pay, date, deposit,**
and so on, to see if they can recognize these words in a different context. This is the story he uses.

I went to the bank today.
There was a big line-up.
I waited in the lineup for thirty minutes.
Finally I got to the teller.

> "I want to deposit this cheque, please."
> "You can't deposit this."
> "Why not?"
> "We can't pay you on this. There's no date on it."
> "I'll put the date on it", I said.
> "We still can't pay you."
> "Why not?"
> "There's no signature on it."

David reminds the class about the incident, retelling the story for one student who was absent in the last class. He gives the students a few minutes (quietly) with the story, to see if there are any parts they recognize, before he reads it aloud for them. Then he reads it aloud twice, sliding his finger along under the words as he says them. He asks members of the class to volunteer if they can read any of the parts. As each part is deciphered David underlines it, and reads the sentence aloud, periodically saying, "What have we got so far?" and reading out the underlined parts. Finally he reads the entire story aloud one more time. Then he gets out scissors and cuts up two copies of the story into sentence strips. He gives each half of the class one set of strips and asks them to reconstruct the story. One group decides to do this by having everyone read their line aloud. The other group works by lining up the strips in order, referring back to the original story. This brings the second lesson to a close, but David realizes that the less advanced group never had a chance to work on deposit slips. He decides that in the next lesson he will use a buddy system, getting the students who have filled out deposit slips to explain the procedure to the others.

EXAMPLE THREE: A COMMUNITY COLLEGE CLASS

Type of class. A group of eighteen students are in a pre-ESL class focussing largely on literacy. The students attend classes every day for five hours. The students are all refugees from either San Salvador or Southeast Asia. There are ten male students and eight female, and ages range from 18 to 54.

Literacy level. All the students are at a very basic level, in terms of English-language literacy. Some are semi-literate in their own language; one is fully literate in Chinese. At least five have no literacy skills in any language.

Language level. Most of the students speak no more than a few words of English. Three class members have some basic oral skills.

Ian, the teacher, has been working with this group of students for only a few days, one day of which was largely taken up with registration procedures. He has done some work on letter and number recognition but has concentrated mostly on using oral work to set up a relaxed, happy atmosphere in the class, which he considers particulary important in view of the refugee background and recent arrival of all these students.

In this lesson, Ian wants to consolidate the students' knowledge of numbers and help them apply that knowledge to money. He also wants to introduce the students to some of the teaching methods he will be using regularly, particularly Total Physical Response and Interview Questionnaires.

Although most of the students do not speak enough English to chat in the normal sense, Ian begins the class by greeting each student individually as the class members drift in. He compliments them on a new piece of clothing or jokes about their expressions, accompanying his remarks with gestures and actions which clarify his meaning. Although many of the students are baffled by his actual words, all appreciate the interest he shows in them and respond with grins and greetings.

When all the students have arrived, Ian holds up one of a large set of cards which he used in a previous lesson to teach numbers. Each card has a numeral and the appropriate number of dots on it, as in this example.

He holds up the different cards one at a time and asks the students to call out the number, chorally at first, later individually. Many of the students are familiar with arabic numbers and can, therefore, concentrate on remembering the English words for them, although they still tend to have to run through the entire sequence, one-two-three-etc., to reach the desired number. Ian encourages them to make quick guesses to try and bypass this process. A few of the students are still unfamiliar with the number forms and are forced to count the dots before they can identify which number is required. At the end of the quick drill, therefore, Ian cuts the cards in half to separate the dots and numerals and gives them to this group of students to re-match and sequence.

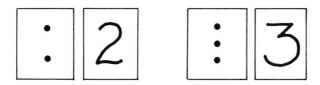

The students do this task in pairs, using a master sheet for reference initially, then working from memory as they find the task becoming easier.

Meanwhile, Ian gathers the rest of the class around him and pulls out a pack of playing cards, using the numbers from 2 to 10 only. He cuts the pack randomly and asks the student on his left to call out the number. Then he hands the pack to the student who has just responded and indicates that he should cut them for his neighbor to identify. Once the students understand what is required he breaks them into small groups of four to five students, gives each group a pack of cards, and sends them off to take turns cutting and asking each other. Ian has deliberately chosen a task very similar to the one he was doing earlier, because he is using this activity to introduce the students to what will be one of his basic teaching techniques — that is, gathering all the students to watch a demonstration of how the small group should perform a task, and then splitting them up to perform the task themselves.

Checking on how each group is handling the task, Ian finds that one group has in it a number of more fluent speakers who find the work very easy. He intervenes there, showing them how to hold two cards together to make a two-digit number for identification.

Once he has seen that the activity is running smoothly, he goes back to the pairs of students who were matching numbers and dots, to see how they are progressing. One pair are still making use of the master chart, and Ian decides that some practice in writing the numbers will help them remember the shapes. He gives them a worksheet which provides an opportunity for both matching and writing.

Name _____

How many?

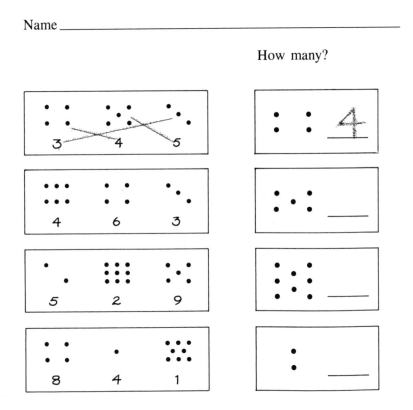

When these students have completed the sheet, Ian brings the whole class together to stand in a circle around a pile of playing cards lying face up on the floor. He chooses one student, saying, "Pablo, give me a 5." Pablo doesn't understand, so Ian bends down, picks up a card with a 5 on it, puts it in Pablo's hand, then stretches out his own hand repeating "Give me a 5." The class soon understand the new phrase "Give me" and they all take turns, helped by some native-language translation when they seem to be having difficulty. Ian has prepared a number of large cards with this command written on them, followed by a numeral. He chooses one, shows it to the students and reads it aloud simultaneously, encouraging the students to respond by picking the appropriate card from the pile. When he shows the next card, "Give me a 4," he pauses before reading it aloud to allow the students to work it out for themselves. Soon he is simply showing the cards without reading them aloud. In this first introduction to Total Physical Response, Ian is limiting the number of commands until he is sure that the students are at ease with the method, introducing variety initially only with the change in numeral.

Once it appears that the class is confident with this procedure, Ian feels that he can introduce one alternative command as a way of focussing the students' attention on the words, not simply the numbers, on the card. He therefore writes up a few instruction cards: "Take a 3," "Take a 6," and so on.

He adds an extra pack of cards to the pile on the floor so that there will be enough of each number for most of the students to take one. Then he introduces the new command, first orally, then with the instruction cards. Soon the students are scrambling to grab the appropriate number as Ian holds up the instruction cards. By having the students display the cards face up, Ian can check visually that they have all chosen correctly.

After a little while, Ian introduces one of the original instruction cards, "Give me a 6" rather than "Take a 6." Some of the students don't notice the change, provoking some good-natured laughter. Soon, however, the class sorts out the two sets of instructions and Ian picks cards at random for a few minutes more.

By now the class is ready for a change of activity, so Ian sets up an interview exercise. Each student is given a class list headed by a single question which he or she must ask of all the other class members. In keeping with the focus on numbers, the question is "What's your telephone number?" (See fig. 15.)

The students spend about fifteen minutes on this activity, walking around the class, finding out the name of any class members they don't know and writing or copying the appropriate phone numbers. Most of the students cannot read the names of their class mates, but get by with gestures, asking each other to point out their names. One student still does not recognize her own name, so Ian makes a point of checking that each student has his or her own number right. Not all the students have telephones, of course, but all have an emergency number — of a landlord, relative, or neighbor — which they have learned.

Most of the students really enjoy this opportunity to move around the room and get to know one another, and there is a fair amount of conversation in the native languages. This doesn't worry Ian. There are enough different language groups that all the students have to resort to English with at least half their classmates, and this provides ample language practice of the item in question. A couple of students remain

Name _____

What's your telephone number?

Pablo   _____

Li Mai   _____

Bounmi   _____

Som Lot   _____   0

Manuel   _____   1 2 3

Maria   _____   4 5 6

Ian   _____   7 8 9

Hourn   _____

Figure 15

seated at first, so Ian encourages them to come along with him while he gets started on completing his own sheet. Once they have the idea, he leaves them to continue alone. He finds that a couple of students are relying very heavily on translators, particularly one of a pair of sisters who is asking no questions for herself but simply copying from her sister. Ian, therefore, takes the less confident sister along with him and encourages her to ask the questions.

When the class members have had time to finish their sheets, they sit down again and check off the answers together. This brings the class to the lunch break, which Ian uses as an opportunity to introduce the use of numbers in expressing time, writing on the board LUNCH 12.00–1.30, accompanied by drawings of the clock face. He will be covering time in more detail in later classes, but wants to make use of such opportunities to put it in a practical context first.

After the lunch break, Ian uses the same physical response method that he used earlier, but changes the cards to read ''Give me 5¢'', ''Take 8¢'', and so on. Once again he introduces the commands orally first, making the students familiar with the language before he introduces the written instructions. A pile of small change replaces the pack of playing cards. Most of the students are already familiar with the new currency, so this session goes more rapidly than the morning session did. Soon Ian has the students in small groups, writing their own instruction cards for other group members.

At this point Ian feels it is time for more oral work, so he joins one group, picks up a few coins, and asks "How much is this?" putting on a puzzled face to indicate the question and carefully counting his coins before announcing the answer. The students soon understand the meaning of the new phrase, and after having them model it chorally and individually he is able to leave them questioning each other while he does the same procedure with the other groups.

For the last forty-five minutes of the class Ian takes the students out for a walk along the street, asking them to identify the numbers on buildings, car license plates, and so on. This also provides the opportunity for some social interaction between the students and helps them get to know each other and feel at home in the class — one of Ian's main objectives.

EXAMPLE FOUR: A COMMUNITY DAYTIME CLASS

Type of Class. This group of twelve women from a public housing estate meet two mornings a week. Many of the women have small children who attend the ESL pre-school provided. The women come from a variety of countries. Ages range from 17 to 45.

Literacy Level. None of the students has had more than a couple of years of education. Some of them know the alphabet but not much more.

Language Level. Very basic. A few students can make themselves understood, but most of them never use English outside the classroom.

Kay, a volunteer teacher, has been working on a theme of food with her students in recent classes, and has built up their oral vocabulary in this area. In the present class, she wants to do an LEA story and get the students practising some basic sentence patterns.

Before the students arrive she hangs up on the walls some food pictures cut from magazines, all clearly labelled. The students drift into the room and look at the pictures, some of them trying out orally the words written underneath. She begins the discussion by asking the students if they like the various foods shown in the pictures. This develops into an informal drill on the lines of "Do you like fish?" "Yes, I do", with the students questioning each other at Kay's direction. Kay then asks the women what they had for dinner the previous night. The more confident students tend to answer first, providing a pattern for less confident ones to follow. When everyone has made some contribution, even if it is only to point to one of the pictures and repeat the word after Kay has read it, she tells the students she is going to write down what they say, and asks for volunteers.

In a language experience story on such a topic, Kay knows that the sentence patterns are likely to be very repetitive, a factor which she hopes will be helpful as the students have such limited literacy skills. She also wants to keep the story short so that the students will find it easy to remember, in the hope that their memory of the content will offset their lack of familiarity with the written symbols. She suspects that the first sentence she writes will probably act as a pattern for the rest of the passage, so she calls on one of the more fluent speakers first. With some help, the following sentence is volunteered: **Last night I eat beef and soup.** Not exactly the perfect sentence Kay had hoped to elicit, but a good enough place to start. She writes down on the flip chart: **My Lan says "Last night I eat beef and soup"**, and reads it back to the class, sliding her finger under the words and checking with My Lan that she has the words right. The next volunteer, Dominica, is a much less fluent speaker, who gets as far as "Last night" before getting stranded. Many of the students offer help, but Dominica still can't seem to get out what she wants to say. Kay decides that if she cannot record Dominica's own words anyway, she may as well at least provide the correct form, so she offers "I had" which the student is happy to accept. She goes on to complete the sentence as **Last night I had fish and rice**. Kay asks for one more volunteer, and ends up with a story which reads:

> My Lan says "Last night I eat beef and soup." Dominica says "Last night I had fish and rice." Yolanda says "Last night I had chicken and rice and fish."

Kay reads each sentence aloud as she writes it and then reads the entire passage twice. As she hoped, there is a lot of repetition in the passage which will help make it easy to remember. The words **beef** and **soup** are not known to some of the students. Kay does a quick sketch of a cow on the blackboard but has problems drawing soup, so falls back on asking the more fluent students to translate.

Once everyone understands what the text is about, Kay asks the students to read along with her as she goes through the passage twice. Then she asks if anyone can find the phrase "Last night". This is quickly done. Kay asks one of the quieter students if she can find the phrase anywhere else in the passage — the first step in recognizing letter clusters rather than relying on memory of the oral words. Picking out such phrases and asking for volunteers to locate them, she covers most of the text. When she then asks the class to read it aloud together, it is noticeable that the less fluent students are much more confident than they were on the first try.

Kay chooses the sentence "Last night I had fish and rice" as the basis for some pattern practice and writes each word on an index card which she arranges along the ledge at the bottom of the blackboard. She asks the students to read the sentence aloud, chorally and individually, then begins covering one word at a time with a blank card, asking them to fill in the missing word. She begins to substitute cards with different food items in the same sentence, using the food items in the story and the ones shown in the pictures on the wall to help comprehension.

At this point Kay puts the students into groups of four and provides each group with the pattern sentence written on cards, which she jumbles up for the group to re-sort. Once this is going smoothly she asks each student to choose one of the food items shown in the wall pictures and to copy its name onto a blank card. These can then be substituted in the sentence. She also provides cards on which the students are to write their names, so that the card sentence can (for example) be amended to read, "Last night My Lan had fish." After the students have worked with the cards for about ten minutes, setting up new sentences and shuffling them for another group member to make sense of, she asks each group to write down two sentences each. Two people in the group will create the sentences and two others will record them on the blackboard, with the help of the creators. Kay asks them to use the board rather than paper, as there are bound to be errors in this first transcription attempt, and it is easier to make corrections on the board.

After the group has read the six new sentences aloud, Kay re-writes the original pattern sentence on the board. She wipes clean one word and hands the chalk over to a student to replace the missing word. In turn each word of the sentence is erased and replaced. At first Kay leaves the students' own sentences (written during the last exercise) on the board for them to copy from, but as the students get more familiar with the sentence she erases the earlier one, thus forcing the women to look closely at the word before Kay wipes it off.

Kay has collected from grocery stores a number of advertisements from which she has cut out illustrations and names of food items. Arranging the students in pairs, she gives one partner a pile of pictures and the other the set of words to be matched with the pictures.

Kay follows up this exercise with a sample worksheet which reinforces the idea but also reviews the phrase "Do you like" covered earlier in the lesson. (See fig. 16.)

By the time this exercise is completed, only about ten minutes are left of class time. Kay uses this time to explain to the students that in an upcoming class she plans to take them to a local supermarket. She would like to have some photographs taken of the trip to be used in later classes for a captioned photo story that the women can develop themselves. (She will use the photographs first of all to promote oral discussion, then let the women select a sequence of pictures which they feel tell the story of the trip. The students will work in pairs to devise captions for each photograph, if necessary dictating the captions to Kay and then copying them out themselves. The pictures and captions can

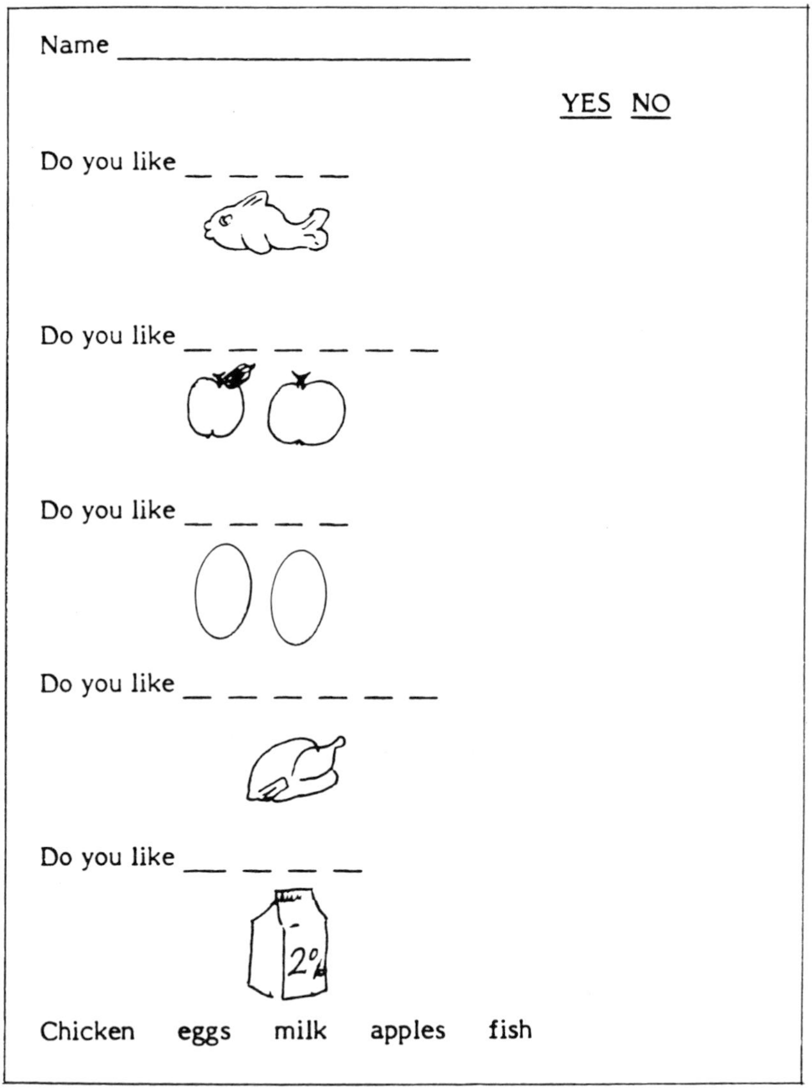
Name ____________________

YES NO

Do you like _ _ _ _

Do you like _ _ _ _ _ _

Do you like _ _ _ _

Do you like _ _ _ _ _ _ _

Do you like _ _ _ _

Chicken eggs milk apples fish

Figure 16

be mounted on a sheet of bristol board to make a complete picture story.) Although Kay is quite competent with a camera she wants the students to be as actively involved as possible, and therefore asks for volunteers to do the photography. Two of the women agree to do this.

Kay deliberately throws open to the women the choice of which supermarket to visit, and also the question of where they could stop for a cup of coffee nearby. Although much of the discussion of these items takes place in the native language, Kay is pleased with the students' participation and feels that they will enjoy the trip more for having done as much of the planning as possible themselves.

In addition to the oral and written vocabulary that the trip will involve, Kay is hoping to use the visit as an introduction to basic map literacy. Accordingly, in her next class she plans to have the students map out their route. During the trip itself she is hoping to have them mark where they find specific food items on a plan of the store. This will involve knowledge of aisle labels and food categories, which she also hopes to cover in the next lesson. As an introduction to this topic, she sets the class a homework task to be done before the next lesson. Each student is to copy down at least two of the large overhead aisle signs in her local supermarket and bring them to the next class, where they can be used as part of a sorting and categorizing activity.

10 / Other Useful Activities

The following are a group of varied activities, all of which work well in a literacy class. They are no substitute for a well-planned curriculum, but provide a way of reinforcing material covered.

Not all of them will be suitable for any particular class, but most of them are adaptable to different content areas and levels, and may stimulate teachers' ideas.

These activities come from a variety of sources, and we are grateful to all the teachers who suggested them.

SORT AND MATCH

A number of useful activities are based on the principle of sorting and categorizing, or sorting and matching. All provide good practice in sight-word recognition; most also help with scanning for significant information.

a. Have two sets of cards, one showing symbols and one showing equivalent written instructions. Give the students or group of students the shuffled cards, asking them to match each symbol with the appropriate written instruction.

b. Collect labels from bottles and cans. Write the generic name of each product on a card. Have students match labels with cards.

c. Collect or photocopy laundry labels. Have students sort labels into **hand washable, dry clean only,** etc. Or, provide written cards saying **HAND WASH, MACHINE WASH,** etc. and have students match each label with the appropriate card.

d. Gather a collection of labels from bottles and cans. Have students sort out poisonous substances from edible ones.

e. Have students group household labels in other ways, entering product name on charts as in the examples.

ASPIRIN

NO SMOKING

BAYER ASPIRIN
FOR RELIEF OF
PAIN AND FEVER:
TAKE 2 TABLETS

 WOMEN

APPLE JUICE

Martins UNSWEETENED
PURE APPLE JUICE
FROM CONCENTRATE
CANADA FANCY

(b)

 NO LEFT TURN

(a)

(e)

FRUITS	JUICES	VEG	CLEANERS
Peaches	V8 Apple	Mushrooms Bean sprouts	Lysol Vanish

Hair spray	Lysol	Oven cleaner

HOUSEHOLD BILLS

a. Photocopy a number of bills for gas, electricity, telephone, etc. Have students work in groups to sort bills by type (e.g., all gas bills together), by date (overdue, due this month, due next month), or by amount (numerical order).

b. Give small groups of students a set of bills and have them complete a chart as in the example.

BILL	AMOUNT	DUE DATE
GAS		
ELECTRICITY		
TELEPHONE		
TELEVISION		

c. Have students match bills with appropriate pre-printed envelopes.

d. Have each student write out a cheque in payment of one of the bills, put cheque plus appropriate return portion of bill into correct envelope, and complete the return address section.

MENUS

Get copies of simple restaurant menus or draw up one of your own based on fast-food chain format (usually block capitals).

a. Have students work in groups to choose the best nutritionally balanced meal for a set price.

b. Encourage skimming by asking, "Do they sell Chinese food?", "Do they have any fresh fruit?", etc.

c. Encourage scanning with questions like "How much is an order of rice?", "What comes with the special dinner?"

d. Draw up a list of questions as in (*b*) and (*c*) above. Put students into teams and see which team can answer all questions most quickly.

POSTMAN

Put the day's worksheets or any other item in envelopes addressed to each student. Give out the envelopes randomly and let each student identify and find the appropriate recipient (i.e., the person to whom the envelope is addressed). (This helps new students get to know each other and also improves their reading skills.)

SELECT AND COMPLETE

To give students some control over the writing process before they can easily formulate their own phrases, give writing assignments of a "select and complete" type, as in the example.

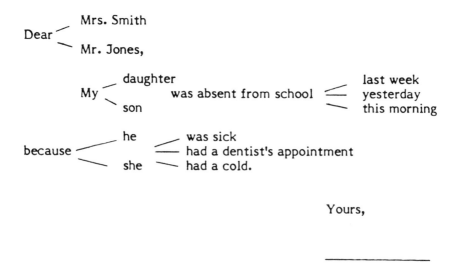

RECOGNIZING WORD SHAPES

Some students find sight words easier if they associate them with a particular shape, e.g.

jump =

Looking at words in this way can also help with correct placement of letters on the lines.

Students can be asked to circle the word having the same shape as
the drawing, e.g.

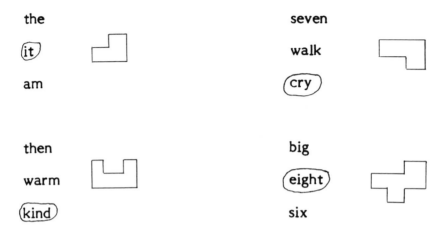

the		seven	
it		walk	
am		**cry**	

then		big	
warm		**eight**	
kind		six	

VISUAL DISCRIMINATION EXERCISES
(Kathleen Troy, Mohawk College)

The type of exercises given to pre-literacy students can be adapted for
more advanced students to help them focus on specific letter patterns.

a) Have students circle the appropriate word for a picture.

	hat	den	
	hit	tin	10
	pat	ten	

b) Provide two columns of phrases and ask students to indicate
whether the pairs are the same or different.

		same	different
live alone	leave alone	_ _ _ _	_ ✓ _ _
payday	payday	_ ✓ _ _	_ _ _ _
full up	pull up	_ _ _ _	_ ✓ _ _

ALPHABETICAL ORDER

a) Letter-to-letter

Put the entire alphabet or sequences of letters scattered over the page.

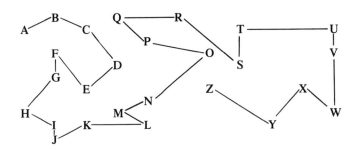

Have students join the letters up in order.

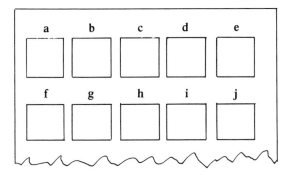

b) Alphabet Slots

Make a master sheet as shown.

Give students, or have students build up on the blackboard, a list of items in a certain category (e.g., food items, articles of clothing, etc.). Have students enter each item under the appropriate letter, as in the example.

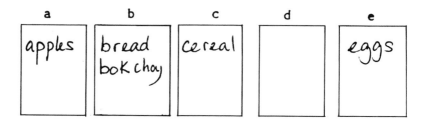

c) *Scrabble Letters:*

Let students work in pairs. Each partner pulls seven scrabble letters at random and sequences them alphabetically. Partner checks that the order is correct.

DIALOGUE JOURNALS
(Bonita Greenbaum)

Dialogue journals take the form of a written conversation between the teacher and individual students. Students each have an exercise book specifically for the dialogue, in which they write anything they would like to say to the teacher. Books are normally given in at the end of class, and the teacher writes a response and returns the book at the next session. A student might write, for instance, "I went out last night" and get the book back with the response, "Did you? Where did you go?"

Rather than correcting errors in the student's work, the teacher can usually phrase a reply to model the correct form. In response to "I go out last night," the teacher might write "I went out last night too. I went to the movies. Where did you go?"

CALENDARS

Provide each student with a sample calendar page, as shown.

a) Ask the students questions, such as "What day is the 21st?", "Is the 26th a Friday?" Have the students question each other.

b) Make up a list of appointments, e.g. "Dentist: Thurs. 24th, 2:00 p.m." Have the students enter these in the appropriate spaces.

SUNDAY	MONDAY	TUESDAY	WEDNESDAY	THURSDAY	FRIDAY	SATURDAY
		1	2	3	4	5
6	7	8	9	10	11	12
13	14	15	16	17	18	19
20	21	22	23	24 Dentist 2:00pm	25	26
27	28	29	30	31		

c) If the students are sufficiently fluent, organize them in pairs, one student in each pair having a partially completed calendar and the other having instructions to arrange a meeting at a time convenient for both. Arrange the dates so that there is only one possible time, as in the example

Student A has:

S	M	T	W	T	F	S
	1	2 Engl. class	3	4 Engl. class	5	6
7	8	9 Dentist 10.00.	10	11	12	13 Sister's wedding
14	15	16 Exam 10.30	17 Exam 1.00	18	19	20 Party 8.00
21	22	23	24	25	26	27
28	29	30	31			

Student B has:

Ask your partner if you can meet

a) Tuesday 9th in the morning

b) Wednesday 17th in the afternoon

c) Thursday 18th in the morning.

TELEPHONE DIRECTORIES

a) Have students work in pairs to find each other's telephone number.

b) Photocopy a page of the directory and have students find particular entries. Choose some entries for which the name alone is sufficient information, others for which an address is needed in order to determine the correct number.

c) Use the Yellow Pages to find the nearest store which sells a given product, the nearest doctor in a certain specialty, and so on.

CATALOGUES AND ADVERTISING FLYERS

a) Have students search flyers for particular items. Have them tell you the price, for example, of the man's coat on page 16, or of the cheapest child's bike in the flyer.

b) Cut illustrations out of the text and have students re-match pictures with text.

c) Get an old catalogue and a current one. Have students compare prices on items appearing in both, and report on price differences. Or use flyers from competing firms, if there is sufficient overlap of content.

WANT-ADS

a) From catalogues, cut some pictures of things like furniture, baby equipment, bikes, etc. Write up short want-ads on index cards describing the items pictured. Have students match pictures with appropriate want-ads. (This is a good exercise for skimming and scanning if pictures are all quite different. It encourages more careful reading if pictures are similar.)

b) Provide extra pictures; have students work in pairs to write related ads, using the set of ads in (a) as models.

GREETING CARDS

For any major holiday, draw up a master for a greeting card. Have students sign cards and send them to other members of the class, school personnel, or their own friends.

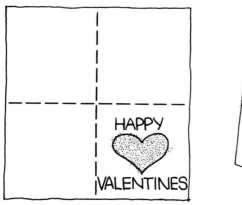

TV GUIDES

   a) Have students circle the programs they watched the previous evening.
   b) Have them mark out an evening's viewing for (i) a western fan, (ii) a sports nut, and (iii) a "sitcom" lover.

CLASS MAP

   a) Hang up a world map. Have students mark their native town or district. Draw colored lines across the map to show the route they travelled to get here. Make a legend showing which colors represent which students.
   b) Get the class to bring in picture postcards of places they have been. Stick the cards on the map at appropriate places. Get students to write (or dictate) captions for the postcards.

OTHER EXAMPLES

The following activities are taken from *ESL Resource Manual, Volume 2*, Intensive ESL and Cultural Orientation Program: Southeast Asia (Center for Applied Linguistics, Washington, D.C., 1982).

The material was developed by the following contributing agencies: the consortium of Save the Children Federation, the Experiment in International Living, and World Education; the International Catholic Migration Commission; Pragmatics International; the Lutheran Immigration and Refugee Service; and the American Council for Nationalities Service.

ALPHABET ORDERING

Purpose	To learn and review letters in alphabetical order.
Number of Players	Small groups of 3-4 players.
Materials	A pack of *alphabet cards* containing 26 letters
Directions	Each group of players is given a complete pack of cards. The cards are dealt out to all the players so that each player has a similar number of cards. The player with M starts and lays the M-card down on the table. Players in turn lay down one card if they have the next one in sequence either forwards or backwards. If they do not have the appropriate card, they lose their turn. If they do have the right card, they continue playing. Eventually, a long alphabet snake should be formed. The winning group is the one that puts all its letters down in order first.

B

Variations

• For reinforcement, players must say the <u>name</u> of the letter. If they say the name incorrectly, they lose their turn and the next player takes his turn.

• The leader puts down two cards, for example, A and C. Players must identify what is missing--B.

• This can be played with number cards.

BINGO

Purpose	To recognize numbers, letters, times, money, words presented orally.
Number of Players	Whole class.
Materials	• A *bingo* card for each player. • Tokens (paper clips, pebbles, coins) in quantity as each player could use up to 23. • Cards that match the symbols on the *bingo* cards.
Directions (For o-100 NUMBER BINGO)	Each player is given a *bingo* card and some tokens. The leader puts all the number cards in a container and pulls them out one-by-one. After each card has been pulled, the leader calls that number out loud. If a player has that number on her *bingo* card, she covers it up with a token. The first player to cover up five numbers in a row (horizontally, vertically, or diagonally) wins. The leader should keep track of all the numbers in order to verify that the player has actually won and not made any mistakes.
Variations	• Times, money, words can be used. • Used a smaller set of numbers and a 2 X 3 grid instead of a 5 X 5 grid. The first player to cover <u>all</u> her numbers wins. Use this variation as an introduction. • Give each player a sheet of paper on which squares have been ruled out (4 X 4 or 5 X 5). On the board, the leader lists either numbers, letters, words, or times-- about 25 to 40--from which each member of the class copies down 16 or 25, one in each empty square. The leader then calls out the numbers, etc. at random, and players cover up the ones they hear with a token. The first to get 4 (or 5) in a row wins.

CONCENTRATION

Purpose	To match like pairs: numbers, letters, time, money, vocabulary.
Number of Players	Two or more.
Materials	Two decks of cards that match, card-for-card.
Directions	All the cards are laid face down on a flat surface. The first player turns up any two cards. If they are a matching pair, she keeps them. If they are not a matching pair, she turns them back face down, and the next player takes a turn and tries to make a pair. The player who makes the most pairs wins.
Variation	● The player must <u>say</u> the word (letter, number, time, amount of money) correctly in order to keep the pair.

CROSSING OUT

Purpose	To recognize numbers, letters, times, money, vocabulary.
Number of Players	One or more.
Materials	Blackboard and chalk; paper and pencils.
Directions	The leader writes down a set of numbers on the blackboard or on paper. (This can also be done on an individual student worksheet.) The students are instructed to cross out, for example, all the 7s. The student who does it first, and accurately, wins.
Variation	Letters, times, money, and vocabulary can be used instead of numbers.

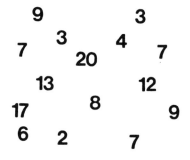

PICTURE STORIES

Purpose	To reinforce left-to-right and top-to-bottom eye movement for beginning readers.
Number of Players	One or more.
Materials	Blackboard and chalk; paper and pencil.
Directions	The teacher draws a story with a minimum of three scenes. The topic could be as common as "My Morning" or as complicated as a story describing writing and mailing a letter. The drawings should be simple and clear. Stick-figures are OK. The drawings should be "read" from left-to-right and from top-to-bottom. After drawing his story, the teacher tells it and then invites the class to tell him back his story. While the students are retelling the story, the teacher should not correct their language, but rather help them when they ask for help. One student could describe one frame, another the next, and so on. Or, the whole class could collectively describe the story. The next step is to ask the students to draw their own story and then to tell it. If students want to know how to write some of the words, the teacher can write them down; but this should not be overdone.

RING A NUMBER

Purpose	To practice numbers.
Number of Players	Whole class divided into two teams.
Materials	Blackboard and chalk, preferably colored chalk.
Directions	Various numbers are written clearly on the board. (The numbers used depend on which numbers the players need practice with.) There are two teams. One member from each stands at the board, each with a different color of chalk in hand. The leader stands at the side and calls out one of the numbers. The two opposing team players look for it, and the first to put a ring around it scores a point. Those at the board should be replaced after 3 numbers. The winning team has the most numbers circled.

```
4          21
    16            45
32
         5    8
30
    9    28     17
  2    54      6
```

Variation	● In place of numbers, there could be letters, clock times, digital times, weights and measures, dates, telephone numbers, sums of money, or vocabulary.

11 / Assessment

Measuring the competence of ESL literacy students is not a simple task, as there are a number of parameters to be considered. First, we would ideally like information about the degree of literacy which students have achieved in their native language, so that we know which skills have to be learned "from scratch" and which skills may be transferred. Secondly, we need to judge the amount of oral English that stude possess, if we are to determine whether reading and writing problen. arise from the mechanics of the process or from problems with unknown language items. Third, we need to measure their literacy skills in English. Because progress in reading and writing may not proceed at the same rate, we will need to break this area down into *comprehension, decoding,* and *writing*.

Before considering methods of evaluating students, we need to look at our reasons for performing assessment. There is little to be gained by merely classifying students, and we particularly want to avoid classifications based on elementary school grade levels. To say an adult reads at the grade 2 level, for instance, is to ignore the wider experience and the more highly developed thinking strategies of the mature student. Such a person may well have a sight vocabulary of a size comparable to that of a grade 2 child, but the way in which the adult makes use of that knowledge is very different.

The major purposes of assessment in adult literacy are placement, diagnosis, and progress evaluation. When we first meet students we may need to make the decision as to which class will best suit their needs — a basic-level ESL class, an ESL literacy class, or an adult basic education class, for example. Some form of assessment will enable us to place students more accurately and rapidly.

When we are actually working with students, assessment is necessary to diagnose the specific areas in which our students need help, to pinpoint the student whose weak listening skills are interfering with reading, or the student whose excellent decoding skills are masking poor comprehension.

Finally, we need to evaluate progress to ensure that our teaching methods are proving successful for each student. It may be that we need to modify our program and use different approaches, to make the program more challenging or to slow it down a little. This type of assessment is evaluating the teacher as much as the students, and is the only way we have of checking that we are doing the best possible job.

Not all assessment will take the form of formal tests. Much of it can be carried out informally on a day-to-day basis as we observe how students cope with tasks and review their results. One thing that we must formalize for ourselves, however, is exactly what skills and abilities we are trying to measure. To help us make the decision regarding placement for instance, we might draw up a checklist of the basic skills a student needs in order to cope with an adult basic education (A.B.E.) class, and see whether our students can meet those requirements. To measure progress, we need to ask ourselves what goal we had in mind for the students at a particular point in the teaching — perhaps ability to cope with shopping in the supermarket, to recognize the letters of the alphabet, or to write a cheque. If lessons are planned with a goal clearly in mind, the measurement of progress is fairly easy. When we consider in detail the methods of assessment, we will find that in some areas the content to be tested is so specific that we need to develop special methods for that area (e.g., for measuring native-language literacy and pre-literacy skills). In other areas, such as measuring students' progress, diagnosing problems, and assessing for placement, there is a much greater overlap of content, and it is therefore useful to consider a type of approach which may be valid for all these purposes. We will therefore look at the ways in which teachers can test students informally over the long term, and at more formal ways (carried out at specific points in the learning process) which provide a written record of achievement.

MEASURING LITERACY IN THE NATIVE LANGUAGE

Because our teaching methods will be different with students who are literate in their own language and those who are not, it is very helpful to get some sense of their ability in this area. Because students frequently bring along an interpreter when they first register, there may be useful information, made available from the students' record sheets from the home country, which the students are not able to offer orally: the record sheet may, for instance, ask for the degree of education reached in the native country. While interpreted interviews and school record sheet data are by no means perfectly reliable sources of information, they can give some help. A student who has attended school only to grade 3 may have learned to read fluently but is unlikely to have done so. A student who has gone on to secondary school can safely be assumed to be literate. At the very least, the record sheet should give information about the native language, so that we can identify students who may be familiar with the roman alphabet. (This information is not always easy to get orally from the students, as teachers who have dealt with large numbers of Southeast Asian refugees will know. Frequently students who identify themselves as coming from Viet Nam — leading the teacher to assume they are familiar with the roman alphabet — are in fact Chinese speakers.)

The use of interpreters is also valuable for gaining information about a student's level of native-language literacy. Professional interpreters are not often available; but it may be possible to borrow a student, from a more advanced class, who can ask new students to write their name and address on a short form prepared in the native language. Students' performance on this task can give a rough gauge of their native-language literacy skills.

Failing these possibilities, the teacher can fall back on using a prepared test. With the help of various community agencies, it should be possible to get short passages, perhaps ten lines, written in the native languages, together with a phonetic transcription of each. The student can then be asked to read the passage aloud while the teacher follows the phonetic transcript. Without any knowledge of the language at all, the teacher can judge, from the fluency of the response and the number of pauses and hesitations, whether the student can decode the text. This does not, of course, measure ability to get meaning from the text, but it can nonetheless give the teacher valuable information.

If the teacher is not entirely sure which language the student speaks, the last method should be avoided. Instead, the teacher might gather some reading material in a variety of languages, and let the students look through them as a group to see if they recognize their own language in the samples provided. Good sources for such multi-language materials are often flyers and booklets put out by the government for newcomers. In Ontario, for instance, the book *Newcomers Guide to Services in Ontario* is available in 23 languages, including most of the Southeast Asian languages which are most difficult for teachers to identify. Another useful source for the major Southeast Asian languages is the CAL/ERIC publication, *Indochinese Students in U.S. Schools* (Language in Education Series No. 42, 1981),[1] which includes, in a number of languages, the brief form shown on pages 124-125.

LITERACY EVALUATION

LAST NAME _____ First Name _____ Middle Name _____

(Khmer)

français
(French)

Directions: Répondez aux deux questions suivantes en français. Puis, si possible, répondez aux mêmes questions en d'autres langues qui se trouvent aussi sur cette carte.

1. Comment vous appelez-vous? _____

2. Vous venez de quel pays? _____

(Thai)

Hmong (Hmong)

Lus tshaj tawm: kom teb cov teebmeem hauv qab no ua lus hoob. tom qab, yog
koj teb tau kom teb cov teebmeem uas pom hauv no ua lwm yam lus.

1. koj lub npe hu li cas?

2. koj nyob qhov twg tuaj?

ລາວ (Lao)

1. ?

2. ?

Tiếng Việt (Vietnamese)

Lời Chỉ Dẫn: Trả lời hai câu hỏi dưới đây bằng tiếng Việt. Sau đó, nếu có
thể, trả lời những câu hỏi trên thẻ này bằng các ngoại ngữ khác.

1. Em tên họ là gì?

2. Em từ đâu tới?

中文 (Chinese)

指示：請用中文回答下列兩個問題。如可能，請用卡也ㄴ其他語言回答其他問題。

1. 你卑姓名？

2. 你從那裏來？

ASSESSING PRE-LITERACY SKILLS

The pre-literacy skills that a student needs for beginning reading and writing can be fairly easily identified, and can be used as a checklist both to diagnose weak areas and to provide guidance in placement. In his article "Literacy Training for Limited English Speaking Adult Learners"[1] Wayne Haverson suggests the following checklist.

PRE-READING CHECKLIST

1. Listening Skills

    _____ Commands (hearing and following)

    _____ Hearing phonemes (connecting sounds and letters)

    _____ Auditory discrimination (understanding and recognizing same sound)

    _____ Auditory perception skills

    _____ Demonstrate understanding and use of passive survival vocabulary

    _____ Demonstrate understanding and use of active vocabulary

2. Sound-Symbol Recognition

    _____ Knowing that oral speech can be written

    _____ Matching symbols

    _____ Recognizing symbols

3. Motor Skills

    _____ Left to right

    _____ Top to bottom

    _____ Having fine motor skills

    _____ Having large motor skills

---

1. In *Teaching ESL to Illiterate Adults*, Adult Education Series 9 (Washington, D.C.: Center for Applied Linguistics, 1980).

_____ Eye-hand coordination

_____ Following on a line

_____ Recognizing upper and lower case letters

_____ Letter formation

4. Visual-auditory Coordination

_____ Using correct word order

_____ Using correct punctuation

5. Visual Perception

_____ Categorizing (same, different)

_____ Recognizing different sizes and styles of type

_____ Recognizing punctuation marks

_____ Recognizing colors

_____ Recognizing shapes

_____ Picture identification (name things in pictures)

_____ Recognizing that a picture represents a real thing

_____ Recognizing sight words

_____ Following top to bottom

_____ Following left to right

_____ Following hand signals

6. Ability to Manipulate Language

_____ Sentence recognition (statement, question)

_____ Producing intonation patterns

_____ Function words

_____ Attention span (concentration)

_____ Using and developing memory

7. **Emotional Readiness**

_____ Can he/she work in a group?

8. **Psychological Readiness**

_____ Self-concept

9. **Physical Readiness**

_____ General health

_____ Sight

_____ Hearing

10. **Other**

_____

_____

_____

Haverson suggests that to measure the students' ability in these areas, we consider competencies, or small tasks demonstrating the appropriate skill. To assess the students' familiarity with left-right progression, for instance, he suggests:

1. Given a picture story of three or more pictures in left to right sequence, learner can point to correct picture as story is told.
2. Given three pictures learner can sequence them from left to right as story is told.
3. Given a symbol at the left of a page and a series of symbols aligned across the page, learner can mark the same symbol.

If we suspect that a student does in fact have all the pre-literacy skills, it is obviously not necessary to test in all these areas. We might instead offer the very simple test of asking a student to copy a short piece of writing onto lined paper. We will see immediately whether the student

a. can follow oral directions
b. has any sense of left-right top-bottom progression
c. has adequate fine muscle control

d. can recognize and match shapes
e. understands placement of letters on the line
f. can form letters.

In addition, we will gain information from the speed and accuracy which the student demonstrates.

MEASURING PROGRESS

In order to make any valid assessment of a student's progress in literacy, we need to have a clear idea in mind of the goals and objectives of our teaching. The general statement that our students are reading better now than they were at the beginning of our classes does not necessarily tell us that they have made the best progress possible in that time. We need to consider carefully what we set out to achieve in our classes if we are to measure their success. Not all teachers will have the same goals in mind. One teacher may plan to have students familiar with the letters of the alphabet by point x, able to read 25 sight words by point y, and able to break words into syllables by point z. Another teacher may define as goals: being able to write name and address, fill in a deposit slip, and find a telephone number in the directory. It is important, however, that we decide what our goals are if we are to measure progress.

Informal Procedures

Assessment need not take the form of a written test. The teacher's daily observation of the students is often a valuable assessment tool. For adult students, attitude and motivation are so important that we can get valuable feedback from the regularity of attendance and the amount of interest displayed. The student who frequently misses classes and rarely seems to concentrate on the material does not need to be tested for the teacher to know that the approach being used is less than adequate.

Simply talking to adult students can be a valuable test. How do they feel about the classes? What types of reading do they want to cover? Are they finding that the material they cover in class is useful outside? What kinds of activities do they feel are of greatest benefit? Does the teacher do anything that they feel is a waste of time?

Reviewing work done by the students over perhaps a three-month period is another useful assessment method. If students have kept a file of language experience (LEA) stories produced in class, do they find it easy to go back and read early stories, or have they forgotten what was covered three weeks ago? If they are learning vocabulary by a sight-word method, can they recognize those words out of context? How does their written work of three months ago compare with their current writing? Can they tell the difference between the two, or are the same mistakes still being made?

Periodically the teacher needs to pause and review the students' progress to date in order to diagnose weak spots which have gone undetected. It is very easy when teaching to a specific objective to fail to notice that a particular student is continually making a certain error. It may take the form of a handwriting problem — making a loose loop for **i** and confusing it with **e**, for instance; or a reading problem — as when a student overrelies on the intial consonant of a word for guidance and happily produces any word beginning with the correct letter, irrespective of the context. It may be an underlying listening problem — the student having problems hearing the difference between certain sounds. Students may consistently demonstrate all these problems and many more. No teacher wants to try to track down all these points halfway through some interesting work on using the transit system, but they should not be left indefinitely. The teacher needs to look at the students' work over a period of time, identify the problems which recur over and over, and then devote some lesson time to working on them.

More Formal Procedures

If we are testing to determine student placement, we need a more objective test scale than we would use in assessing our own program. The test scale might be used for initial placement or to decide whether students are ready to move on to another class. Class levels vary from one institution to another, but, for most people working in adult ESL literacy, the main goal is to bring students to the point where they can participate in a regular ESL class which reflects their oral ability. We can therefore get some sense of the level they need to reach if we look at the reading and writing material they will face in the early stages of the new class.

Normally that level will demand at least the following skills and abilities:

1. Recognize, name, and produce the letters of the alphabet. Know the sounds normally associated with each letter.
2. Recognize, understand, and produce numbers to 10.
3. Fill in a simple form requiring name, address, and telephone number.
4. Have as sight vocabulary most of the 200 most common words in English (see Appendix A).
5. Have word-attack skills to attempt new words, using sound-symbol correspondence, context clues, etc.
6. Understand the concept of a sentence, and basic punctuation marks such as comma, period, and question mark.

7. Be able to copy written text.
8. Feel sufficiently confident with print to attempt to read and write previously unknown words.

Of the tests available commercially, only a very few are likely to be useful to the ESL literacy teacher. One of these is the BEST test (Basic English Skills Test) from the Center for Applied Linguistics. This test has a literacy component focussing on such survival tasks as reading price labels and writing cheques. Another is the HELP Test (Alemany Press) which is designed specifically for students with low oral skills and low literacy skills. A third test, the Ann and Ben Listening Test (Oregon Indochinese Refugee Vocational ESL Program), while intended mostly for listening comprehension, also measures visual discrimination of pre-literacy students.[3]

Most of the other tests commercially available are of very limited use. The majority of standardized reading tests are intended for children and use material inappropriate for adults. Most tests designed for adult literacy are of limited use as they are intended for native speakers and employ language which ESL students are unlikely to know. For example, one test requires the students to identify which item in a series of pictures begins with the letter **b**. The pictured objects include a basket, a bucket, a door knob, and a baby. Most ESL students would have only the last item in their vocabulary. Another problem with most tests is that, since they are designed to measure people who have had a number of years of literacy training, their focus is on a relatively high degree of literacy skill. They measure, for instance, the student's ability to answer comprehension questions based on fairly complex passages, or their recognition of the main idea in a text. Most ESL literacy students would have difficulty even in following the instructions on such tests.

A further complication is the cultural bias shown in tests designed for native speakers. It is extremely difficult on such tests to determine whether a student's low score reflects problems with literacy or failure to recognize the cultural implications.

Finally, of course, most such tests tend to be developed for the purpose of classification, rather than as a way of pinpointing the students' weak areas.

For all these reasons it is unlikely that teachers will find most commercially available tests to be very useful to them, and will prefer to develop their own assessment procedures. One book which could serve as a useful model is *How's It Going?: An Alternative to Testing Students in Adult Literacy* by Martin Good and John Holmes (Adult Literacy Unit, Surrey, 1978). This book, which is addressed to both literacy teachers and students, includes some excellent charts breaking down progress in reading and writing into small measurable units, as shown in the reduced examples on pages 132 and 133.

Reading

TONY

KEY TO SYMBOLS

A = attitude
S = skill
K = knowledge

GRADES

✓ = knows it, is aware of it at this level
O = is working at it, within this level
X = at this level, hasn't started yet

ARROW 1

Do you use reading with a sense of purpose? For real things you need like TV guides, labels, etc. as well as just wanting to learn to read? And without feeling too nervous even to have a go? Can you cope with parts of 'Write First Time', 'This Month' and some newspapers? (We mean can you get the gist of some articles with a little help?) Do you know the techniques you use to help you read, and how to combine them? Like guessing, seeing at a glance, sounding out? Do you know most of the letter sounds that start words? The ordinary ones like 'T in table' etc? And can you sometimes use them to help you guess the rest? Do you know most of the Social Sight words you need (like 'Danger', 'Exit', 'Street', 'Push' etc.)? And can you read without getting stuck on words like 'and', 'but', 'the', etc?

Can you say 'Yes' to most of that? If so, you're 'Not Bad'. If not, you're 'Beginning'.

ARROW 2

Can you read fluently most of the time? Can you tell someone else about what you've read? And give your views on it? Do you know what's available in the library? Can you use some reference books? And do you know where to find them? Or at least, how to find out? If not, can you ask for help without feeling embarrassed? Do you deal with everyday reading almost automatically (like receipes, DIY books, instructions, official forms, letters, kids' stories, adult stories, magazines)? Can you glance at a newspaper and see what interests you? Then read the bits that you like the look of? Do you feel 'In charge' of the whole business?

Can you say 'Yes' to most of that? If so, you're reading 'With Ease'.

Key	Things to do	BEGINNING						NOT BAD						WITH EASE					
		Date	Grade	Date	Grade	Date	Grade	Date	Grade	Date	Grade	Date	Grade	Date	Grade	Date	Grade	Date	Grade
A	Reading is communication	1/77	X	5/77	✓	11/77	✓	1/78	✓	5/78	✓								
A	Reader's job (Voice)		X		✓		O		O											
SK	Alphabet		O		✓		✓													
SK	Social Sight		O		O		O													
SK	'Key' words		X		O		✓													
ASK	Context cueing		O		O		✓		O		✓									
SK	Visual features		O		O		✓		✓		✓									
SK	Letter names		O		O		✓													
SK	Phonics		O		O		✓		✓		✓									
ASK	Failure technique		X		✓		✓		✓		O									
AK	Idea of strategy		X		✓		✓		O		✓									
AK	Purposes		X		O		O		X		O									
K	Print 1: L & R		✓		✓		✓													
SK	Print 2: Structure		X		O		O		O		O									
ASK	Grammatical jargon		X		✓		✓		O		O									
SK	Dictionary		X		O		O		X		O									
ASK	Study skills						✓		X		X									
ASK	Skim/Scan		X		O		O		X		X									
ASK	Library		X		O		O		X		O									
SK	Speed		X		O		O		X		O									

Reading Strategy

Writing

TONY

KEY TO SYMBOLS

A = attitude
S = skill
K = knowledge

GRADES

✓ = knows it, aware of it at this level
O = is working at it, within this level
X = starting off at this level

ARROW 1

Do you use writing with a sense of purpose? For real things (like notes to the milkman or messages, as well as just wanting to learn to write or spell? Do you know about making drafts and correcting them? Can you tell when it's important to spell perfectly and when it's not? Do you write to friends and relatives without worrying? And do you know address and words like 'road' 'street', 'avenue'? Can you fill in easier forms (like Driving Licence Application, Child Benefit Scheme, Giro) on your own? How about cheques? Are you confident about doing those even when others can see you (like in the Post Office or a shop)? Do you have a good way of remembering spellings you want? Can you use simpler dictionaries to check spellings or meanings? Do you have a home-made one? And have you noticed some things about how English spelling works (like the way 'hit' becomes 'hitting')? Do you keep an address book? Are you happy about using full stops and capital letters? Do you ask people how to spell words you're not sure of? And do you sometimes write just for yourself?

Can you say 'Yes' to most of that? If so, you're 'Not Bad'. If not, you're 'Beginning'.

ARROW 2

Do you feel confident about writing whenever you have to? Or want to? Can you fill in hard forms like insurance proposals or job applications without much help? Or ask for help when you need it without feeling embarrassed? Can you use a big dictionary? Do you know words a lot about how English spelling works? For example, prefixes, suffixes, words with 'gh' in them? Do you feel confident about using commas, semi-colons, paragraphs? Do you keep your papers in a filing system? Can you write formal letters if you have to, like to the Bank, the local authority, the council? And can you use other styles too, for example in stories or personal letters? Do you sometimes use writing to help sort out your thoughts? If you have to write for your job, can you do it? Or for a course? Without worrying so much that it gets in the way? Can you take useful notes? And is your handwriting fairly readable and fast? Can you often tell when you've made a spelling mistake? Do you feel in charge of it all?

Can you say 'Yes' to most of that? If so, you're writing 'With Ease'.

Key	Things to do	BEGINNING Date	Grade	Date	Grade	Date	Grade	NOT BAD Date	Grade	Date	Grade	Date	Grade	WITH EASE Date	Grade	Date	Grade	Date	Grade
A	Writing is communication	9/77	O	1/78	✓	5/78	✓	1/78	✓	5/78	✓								
A	Voice	9/77	✓					5/78	✓										
SK	Form letters	9/77	O	1/78	✓														
SK	Grammatical conventions	9/77	O	1/78	O	5/78	O												
AK	Purposes	9/77	O	1/78	O	5/78	O												
AK	Drafts	9/77	X	1/78	X	5/78	X												
AS	Editing	9/77	X	1/78	X	5/78	O												
ASK	Failure technique	9/77	O	1/78	O	5/78	O												
SK	Memorising		O		O		O												
SK	Dictionary		O		O		O												
ASK	Noticing		O		O		O												
AK	Concept of strategy		O		✓		✓												
SK	Writing letters		X		X		O												
AK	Importance of practice		✓		✓		✓												
ASK	Knowing about the language		O		✓		✓												
SK	Note taking		O		✓		✓												
SK	Essays							5/78	O										
ASK	Writing for speech																		
SK	Thesaurus																		

Writing Strategy / Spelling Strategy

How's It Going? is intended for native speakers, but the focus on conquering individual strategies and techniques makes it much more adaptable to second-language learners than tests in which the student is asked to demonstrate competence with given language. ESL teachers will probably want to adapt the charts to include sections on listening skills, understanding of sentence structure, and so on. The basic approach, however, of determining which skills and attitudes we aim to teach, and working in consultation with the student to measure progress, is one which can be useful with all students. It not only provides the teacher with a clear record of progress, but demonstrates this progress to the students, who otherwise may not realize how much their skills have improved.

The individualized nature of such an approach is also valuable to a teacher who has a wide variety of students in the class. Adult students are frequently skilled at hiding their shortcomings in literacy, and their defence mechanisms may operate in the classroom. It is difficult to be the one student to stand up and admit to not understanding the teacher's point. The temptation is to nod and smile and feign understanding, especially if more advanced students are vocal in their comprehension. Soon the weight of material not understood becomes so heavy that the student cannot possibly follow subsequent lessons, and falls back more and more on attempting merely to cover up lack of knowledge. Only constant review of individual progress can alert the teacher to this situation.

12 / Resources

STUDENT LITERACY MATERIALS

Beal, Kathleen Kelly. *Entry to English.* Austin, Tex.: Steck Vaughn, 1982.

Boyd, John, and Boyd, Mary Ann. *Before Book One.* New York, N.Y.: Regents, 1982.

Longfield, Diane M. *Passage to ESL Literacy.* Arlington Heights, Ill.: Delta Systems Inc. 1981.

Mrowicki, Linda, and Furnborough, Peter. *A New Start Literacy Workbook I.* Exeter, N.H.: Heinemann Educational Books, 1982.

Mullins, Carol. *Life Skills Reading.* New York, N.Y.: Educational Design Inc., 1980.

Wigfield, Jack. *First Steps in Reading and Writing.* Rowley, Mass.: Newbury House, 1982.

OTHER CLASSROOM MATERIALS USEFUL FOR LITERACY CLASSES

de Garcia, Karen B., and Nixon, Barbara H. *Discovering English.* Rowley, Mass.: Newbury House, 1982.

Foley, Barbara, and Pomann, Howard. *Lifelines Book I.* New York, N.Y.: Regents Publishing Co., 1981.

Mosenfelder, Donn, and Kaplan, Ellen. *Lifeskills Writing.* New York, N.Y.: Educational Design Inc., 1981.

Mrowicki, Linda, and Furnborough, Peter. *A New Start: Students Book.* Exeter, N.H.: Heinemann Educational Books, 1982.

MATERIALS OF INTEREST TO TEACHERS

Adult Basic Literacy Curriculum and Resource Guide. Victoria, B.C.: Province of British Columbia, Ministry of Education, n.d.

Asher, James A. *Learning Another Language Through Actions: The Complete Teacher's Guidebook.* Los Gatos, Cal.: Sky Oaks Productions, 1977.

Bernstein, Judith. *People, Words and Change.* Algonquin College, March 1980, Ottawa. (Mimeo).

Carroll, John B., and Chall, Jeanne S. (eds.). *Toward a Literate Society.* New York, N.Y.: McGraw Hill, 1975.

Colvin, Ruth J., and Root, Jane. H. *READ: Reading Evaluation — Adult Diagnosis.* Syracuse, N.Y.: Literacy Volunteers of America, 1982.

Colvin, Ruth J., and Root, Jane. H. *TUTOR: Techniques Used in the Teaching of Reading.* Syracuse, N.Y.: Literacy Volunteers of America, 1981.

ESL Literacy Resource Guide. Illinois Statewide ESL/Adult Education Service Center, Nov. 1982, Arlington Heights, Ill. (Mimeo).

Freitag, Aloyse, and Weber, Doris. *An Experiment in Literacy with Adult Immigrants.* Province of Quebec, Ministry of Immigration, Oct.1980. (Mimeo).

Gibson, Eleanor, and Levin, Harry. *The Psychology of Reading.* Cambridge, Mass.: MIT Press, 1975.

Good, Martin, and Holmes, John. *How's It Going? An Alternative to Testing Students in Adult Literacy.* Adult Literacy Unit, Surrey, 1978. Orders to: Interprint Graphic Services Ltd., Half Moon Street, Bagshot, Surrey, U.K.

Goodman, Kenneth; Goodman, Yetta; and Flores, Barbara. *Reading in the Bilingual Classroom: Literacy and Biliteracy.* Rosslyn, Va.: National Clearinghouse for Bilingual Education, 1979.

Gudchinsky, Sarah. *Handbook of Literacy.* Summer Institute of Linguistics, University of Oklahoma, 1962.

Gudchinsky, Sarah (ed.). *Notes on Literacy.* Summer Institute of Linguistics, Huntington Beach, Cal., n.d.

Gudchinsky, Sarah. *A Manual of Literacy for Preliterate People.* Summer Institute of Linguistics, Huntington Beach, Cal., 1973.

Haverson, Wayne W., and Haynes, Judith. *Literacy Training for ESL Adult Learners.* Washington, D.C.: Center for Applied Linguistics, 1982.

Lee, Doris M., and Allen, R. V. *Learning to Read Through Experience.* Englewood Cliffs, N.J.: Prentice Hall, 1966.

Kavanagh, James F., and Venezky, Richard L. *Orthography, Reading and Dyslexia.* Baltimore, Md.: University Park Press, 1980.

MacFarlane, Tom. *Teaching Adults to Read.* Adult Literacy Resource Agency, Bagshot, Surrey, U.K.

McGee, Donna. *Reading Skills for Basic Literacy.* Vancouver, B.C.: Vancouver Community College, 1977.

McGee, Donna, and Maglaque, Paulette. *Tutor Five Step.* Vancouver,B.C.: Vancouver Community College, 1979. (Mimeo).

Moorhouse, Catherine. *Helping Adults to Spell.* Adult Literacy Resource Agency, Bagshot, Surrey, U.K.

Pulvertaft, Ann. *Carry on Reading.* Ashton Scholastic, Bagshot, Surrey, U.K.

Selman, Mary. *An Introduction to Teaching ESL to Adults.* Vancouver,B.C.: Pampas Press, 1979.

Smith, Frank. *Understanding Reading.* San Francisco, Cal.: Holt, Rinehart and Winston, 1971.

Smith, Frank. *Psycholinguistics and Reading.* New York, N.Y.: Holt, Rinehart and Winston, 1973.

Strauch, Anne Ebersole. *Methods and Materials for ESL Literacy.* Master's thesis, University of California, Los Angeles, 1978.

Teaching ESL to Illiterate Adults. Adult Education Series 9, Language and Orientation Resource Center, Center for Applied Linguistics, Washington, D.C., n.d.

Thomas, Audrey (ed.). *Canadian Adult Basic Literacy Resource Kit.* Movement for Canadian Literacy, July 1979, Toronto, Ont.

Thonis, Eleanor Wall. *Teaching Reading to Non-English Speakers.* London: Collier Macmillan International, 1970.

Unesco. *Practical Guide to Functional Literacy: A Method of Training for Development.* New York, N.Y.: Unesco, 1973.

Wallerstein, Nina. *Language and Culture in Conflict.* Reading, Mass.: Addison Wesley Publishing Co., 1982.

Articles

Batchelor, Karen; Weiss, Monica; and Wigfield, Jack. "ESL Adult Literacy — Some Want to Read." In Donna Ilyin and Thomas Tragardh (eds.), *Classroom Practices in Adult ESL.* Washington, D.C.: TESOL, 1978.

Clark, Mark A. "The Short Circuit Hypothesis of ESL Reading — or, When Language Competence Interferes with Reading Performance." *Modern Language Journal*, vol. 64, no. 2 (Summer 1980), 203-209.

Fries, Charles C. "Learning to Read English as a Part of the Oral Approach." *Journal of the Reading Specialist*, vol. 4, (May 1967).

Goodman, Kenneth S. "Reading: A Psycholinguistic Guessing Game." In Kenneth Croft (ed.), *Readings in English as a Second Language.* Cambridge, Mass.: Winthrop Publishers, Inc., 1972.

Hatch, Evelyn. "Research on Reading a Second Language." *Journal of Reading Behavior*, vol. 4, no. 1 (1974), 53-61.

Haverson, Wayne. "Literacy Training for Limited English Speaking Adult Learners." In *Teaching ESL to Illiterate Adults*, Adult Education Series 9. Washington, D.C.: Center for Applied Linguistics, 1980.

McGee, Donna. "Reading Skills for Basic Literacy." *TESL Talk*, vol. 9, no. 1 (Winter 1978), 53-58. Ministry of Culture and Recreation, Toronto, Ont.

Moriarty, Pia, and Wallerstein, Nina. "Student/Teacher/Learner: A Freire Approach to ABE/ESL." *Adult Literacy and Basic Education*, vol. 3, no. 3 (Fall 1979), 193-200.

Pratt, Sidney. "Using Student Produced Materials: A Report from Britain." *TESL Talk* (Summer 1980), pp. 35-40. Ministry of Culture and Recreation, Toronto, Ont.

Rigg, Pat. "Beginning to Read in English: The L.E.A. Way." *SPEAQ Journal* , vol. 1, no. 3, 60-70.

Thonis, Eleanor W. "Reading Instruction for Language Minority Students." In *Schooling and Language Minority Students: A Theoretical Framework.* Los Angeles, Cal.: University of California, Evaluation, Dissemination and Assessment Center, 1981, pp. 147-181.

Wigfield, Jack. "ESL Adult Literacy." *CATESOL Occasional Papers*, no. 3 (Winter 1976-77), pp. 1-21.

Appendix A / Two Hundred Most Frequently Used Words (in Rank Order)

the	her	two	each	great	upon
of	all	may	just	old	school
and	she	then	those	year	every
to	there	do	people	off	don't
a	would	first	Mr.	come	does
in	their	any	how	since	got
that	we	my	too	against	left
is	him	now	little	go	number
was	been	such	good	came	course
he	has	like	very	right	war
for	when	our	make	used	until
it	who	over	world	take	always
with	will	man	still	three	away
as	more	me	own	himself	something
his	no	even	see	few	fact
on	if	most	men	house	through
be	out	made	work	use	water
at	so	after	long	during	less
by	said	also	get	without	public
I	what	did	here	again	put
this	up	many	between	place	think
had	its	before	both	around	almost
not	about	must	life	however	hand
are	into	through	been	home	enough
but	than	back	under	small	far
from	them	years	never	found	took
or	can	where	day	Mrs.	head
have	only	much	same	thought	yes
an	other	your	another	went	government
they	new	way	know	say	system
which	some	well	while	part	
one	could	down	last	once	
you	time	should	might	general	
where	these	because	us	high	

Appendix B / Common Syllable Patterns in English

1.	-ab (cab)	-ad (bad)	-ag (bag)	-an (can)	-ang (hang)	-ap (cap)	-at (mat)
	-and (stand)	-ank (tank)	-ash (sash)	-ass (mass)			
2.	-eb (web)	-ed (wed)	-eg (leg)	-ell (well)	-en (hen)	-end (lend)	
	-ent (lent)	-ess (dress)	-est (nest)	-et (wet)			
3.	-ib (rib)	-id (kid)	-ig (big)	-ick (wick)	-ill (sill)	-in (pin)	-ip (nip)	-it (sit)
4.	-ub (rub)	-uck (duck)	-ud (mud)	-ug (bug)	-ull (dull)	-um (rum)	-ump (bump)
	-un (bun)	-ung (hung)	-ush (hush)	-ut (but)			
5.	-ob (slob)	-ock (clock)	-od (pod)	-og (hog)	-ong (long)	-ot (cot)	
6.	-ace (pace)	-ade (spade)	-age (cage)	-aid (maid)	-ail (mail)	-ain (pain)	
	-ale (pale)	-ame (name)	-ane (pane)	-ape (cape)	-ate (date)		
	-ave (cave)	-ay (day)	-aze (daze)	-eigh (weigh)			
7.	-ew (few)	-use (fuse)	-ute (flute)	-oot (root)	-oom (boom)	-oon (coon)	-oop (hoop)	-oot (hoot)

8. -oad   -oal   -oam   -oan   -oat   -ode
    (toad)   (coal)   (roam)   (loan)   (coat)   (code)

    -oe   -old   -ole   -olt
    (hoe)   (bold)   (sole)   (colt)

    -one   -ope   -ose   -ote
    (bone)   (rope)   (nose)   (note)

9. -e   -ea   -each   -eak   -eal   -eam
    (me)   (tea)   (peach)   (peak)   (heal)   (seam)

    -ean   -eat   -eed   -ee   -eek
    (mean)   (meat)   (need)   (free)   (week)

    -eep   -een   -eet   -y
    (weep)   (seen)   (beet)   (marry)

10. -ook   -ood   -oot
    (look)   (wood)   (foot)

11. -ice   -ide   -ight   -ike   -ile   -ime
    (mice)   (wide)   (fight)   (bike)   (pile)   (time)

    -ind   -ine   -ire   -ite   -y
    (mind)   (wine)   (tire)   (kite)   (my)

12. -ouch   -out   -ound   -ouse   -own   -ow   -oul
    (pouch) (pout)   (pound)   (mouse) (down)   (cow)   (foul)

13. -oy   -oise
    (boy)   (noise)

14. -ar   -er   -ir   -or
    (star)   (term)   (girl)   (torn)

APPENDIX